# EVALUATION OF OPERATION NEIGHBORHOOD

Peter B. Bloch
David I. Specht

4000-3

December 1973

THE URBAN INSTITUTE

WASHINGTON, D.C.

*This research was conducted under contract with the New York City Police Department, which received a grant for this study from the Law Enforcement Assistance Administration of the United States Department of Justice.*


*This is an evaluation of Operation Neighborhood as of December 1972, the date on which a final report was delivered to the New York City Police Department.*

*REFER TO URI-26000 WHEN ORDERING.*



*ISBN 87766-089-1*
*UI 4000-3*


*Available from*

*Publications Office*
*The Urban Institute*
*2100 M Street, N.W.*
*Washington, D.C.  20037*

74-1917

*List Price:  $3.95*


*A/73/750*

*ACKNOWLEDGMENTS*

This report could not have been completed without the full cooperation of the New York City Police Department, including the assistance of Sergeant Anthony Vastola, Captain Frank Mendyk, Jr., and Captain John Watters. Chief of Patrol Donald Cawley, Inspector Henry Morse, Chief Inspector Michael Codd and Commissioner Patrick V. Murphy showed a continuing interest in our work--for which we are grateful. We also appreciate the cooperation we received from the principals of George Washington High School and Brandeis High School in the administration of the youth portion of our Citizen Survey.

Joseph Wholey, Joseph Lewis, Joe Nay, Garth Buchanan, Philip Schaenman, Robert Sadacca, Bobbie Carlin, Tito dela Garza, and Joseph Gueron of The Urban Institute all contributed analytical or data processing assistance.

Tricia Knapick revised and edited the final version and Jill Bury typed it. Montina Pyndell, project secretary, prepared the initial version of this paper.

*TABLE OF CONTENTS*

TABLE OF CONTENTS (Continued)

## LIST OF TABLES

## LIST OF TABLES (Continued)

*LIST OF TABLES (Continued)*

*LIST OF TABLES (Continued)*

LIST OF TABLES (Continued)

LIST OF CHARTS

INTRODUCTION, CONCLUSIONS AND RECOMMENDATIONS

INTRODUCTION
‾‾‾‾‾‾‾‾‾‾‾‾

In January 1971, New York City launched a neighborhood team policing program called "Operation Neighborhood." At that time, a single precinct was divided so that a sergeant and a team of patrolmen would have twenty-four-hour responsibility for police service in a neighborhood. The objectives of the program, which now includes over 62 teams and over ten percent of all patrol officers, are:

- To control crime more effectively

- To increase community cooperation in crime control

- To improve police-community relations

- To tailor police operations to the needs of local communities

- To increase police officer job satisfaction

- To improve the working relationship between patrol officers and their immediate supervisors.

The goals of neighborhood team policing require substantial change throughout an entire police department. Table 1 presents a summary statement of some of the important changes. Neighborhood police teams (NPTs), as being implemented by New York City, change the roles of patrolmen and supervisors and alter the entire organization of the patrol function. Training, vehicle dispatching, planning, and community relations all are part of the Operation Neighborhood concept.

TABLE 1: IMPORTANT CHANGES IN POLICE METHODS

(Summary Statement)

| OLD METHOD | OPERATION NEIGHBORHOOD |
|---|---|
| 1.  Shift responsibility (eight hour tours with no one other than the precinct commander with any around-the-clock responsibility). | 1.  Team commander has around-the-clock responsibility. |
| 2.  Quasi-military or authoritarian supervision and little or no in-service training. | 2.  Professional supervision with consultation, setting up of objectives, developing an educational program, and understanding the patrol officer's job problems. |
| 3.  Assignment of the first available car to a call for police service--with priority for emergency calls. | 3.  Assignment of neighborhood cars to all non-emergency calls for service. Sending a neighborhood car out of its area only for emergencies that can not be covered by other cars. |
| 4.  Special police units (tactical, detective, etc.) operate in local neighborhoods without informing local patrol officials. | 4.  Special police units inform themselves of neighborhood team goals and, whenever possible, consult in advance with the team commander who is responsible for a local area. |
| 5.  Community relations as "image building" (special units for community relations plus some speaking engagements for officials). | 5.  Community relations as an important function for the team commander and for patrolmen--who design citizen contacts to increase citizen involvement in crime control and to assist the police in meeting local needs for police service. |
| 6.  Reactive policing (wait for calls for service, respond, and occasionally plan in advance for responses). | 6.  Decentralized planning (learning about crime patterns, allocating personnel, developing preventive programs and service activities) and innovation (by delegating authority to sergeants, the number of people with power to innovate is increased). |

Neighborhood police teams operate in an extremely complex world. Chart 1 is an attempt to show visually the complexities, both of the society in which we live and of the police department in which the neighborhood police teams operate. Many of the factors which can influence the success of a policing program are outside the influence of a police department because they are determined by private institutions (social and economic), by other government agencies (e.g., employment and health agencies) or by other parts of the criminal justice system (courts, prosecution or corrections). There also are many units within a police department (e.g., detective or tactical) which can materially affect the success of a neighborhood police team operation.

The goals of neighborhood police teams will be discussed in greater detail in the beginning of each of the subsequent chapters. In this way, the evaluation findings can be discussed in relation to specific goals.

## ORIGINS OF OPERATION NEIGHBORHOOD

In October 1970, Patrick V. Murphy left Detroit to become police commissioner in New York City. The Knapp Commission was about to commence hearings which would publicly document corruption within the New York City Police Department. As a result, the corruption issue occupied a substantial amount of the energies of the commissioner and his department. First, the corruption-investigating units were centralized into a single unit. Second, many personnel changes were made, both within the corruption-investigation units and in the command positions. In fact, by 1972, all of the officials who were precinct commanders when Commissioner Murphy took office had been replaced.

CHART 1: NEIGHBORHOOD TEAM POLICING AS IT EXISTS IN NEW YORK CITY

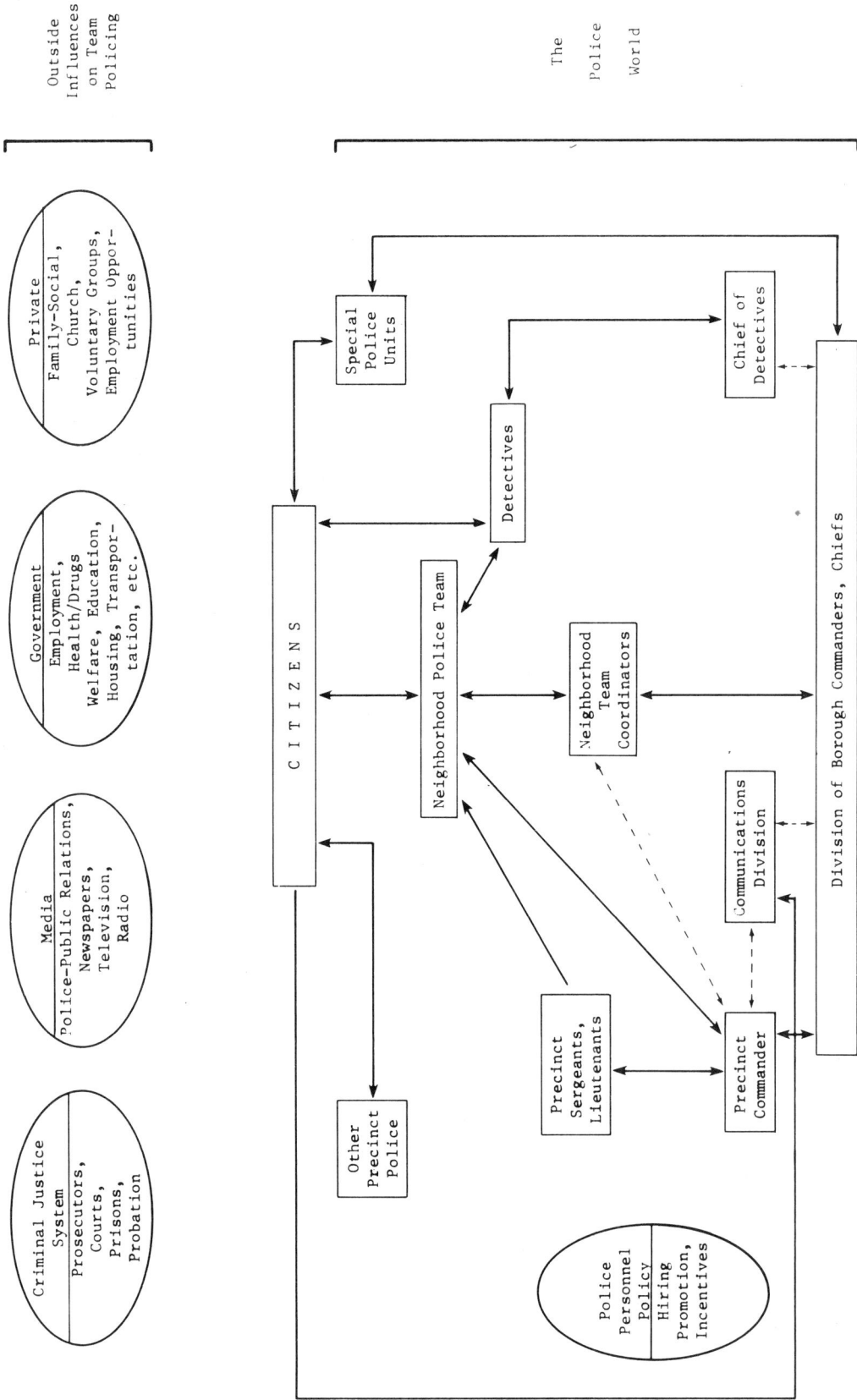

Outside Influences on Team Policing

Criminal Justice System
Prosecutors, Courts, Prisons, Probation

Media
Police-Public Relations, Newspapers, Television, Radio

Government
Employment, Health/Drugs, Welfare, Education, Housing, Transportation, etc.

Private
Family-Social, Church, Voluntary Groups, Employment Opportunities

The Police World

CITIZENS

Special Police Units

Detectives

Chief of Detectives

Neighborhood Police Team

Neighborhood Team Coordinators

Division of Borough Commanders, Chiefs

Communications Division

Precinct Sergeants, Lieutenants

Precinct Commander

Other Precinct Police

Police Personnel Policy
Hiring, Promotion, Incentives

Key: ⟷ Two-way communication, ----- Weak communication, → One-way communication

Commissioner Murphy and his appointees also attacked the lack of police efficiency. Precinct commanders were informed that the precincts were their responsibility and that they would be held accountable for the actions of their men. This entailed responsibility for corruption, issuance of traffic tickets, answering radio calls for service, making arrests, and all other aspects of police service in the precincts. There was a push to put more men on the street and to reduce wasted hands in inside positions. Plainclothes officers were used in a campaign against street crime.

Meanwhile the department had severe budgetary limitations. During Commissioner Murphy's first two years in office, the overall strength of the police department was cut by approximately one-eighth.

These are just a few major problems that Commissioner Murphy had to face. It was in this context that the commissioner decided to implement the team policing concept. The concept was one with which he had experimented in a small way during his tenure as police commissioner in Detroit.

## ORIGINS OF NEIGHBORHOOD POLICE TEAMS

In November 1970, Commissioner Murphy asked his planning division to write an order initiating team policing. That order was constructed primarily by Lieutenant Patrick Murphy[1] of the planning division on the basis of consultations with Peter B. Bloch of The Urban Institute and reference to two publications, "The Beat Commander," by Patrick V. Murphy and Peter B. Bloch (Police Chief, May 1970), and "Comparison of the Beat Commander System to Ordinary Police Operations," by Peter B. Bloch (The Urban Institute, May

---

1.   No relation.

1970). The order, signed by the chief of patrol, was entitled "Operation
Neighborhood--Neighborhood Police Team Program" and was issued December 30,
1970 as T.O.P. 364. (See Appendix A.)

Prior to January 1, 1971, when the first teams went into operation, the
planning division helped select four outstanding sergeants to become the
first team commanders. These individuals were thoroughly briefed in the
concept. They visited other cities where team policing had been implemented.
They then selected their teams from among volunteers in the precincts where
they were assigned as team commanders.

BACKGROUND OF THIS EVALUATION

In December 1970, The Urban Institute was invited by the New York
Police Department to consider conducting an evaluation of the forthcoming
Operation Neighborhood. Police officials hoped that a contract could be
closed quickly and that the work could be commenced. It soon became obvious,
however, that extensive delays would be experienced in seeking funding through
the Law Enforcement Assistance Administration. Moreover, it was discovered
that city regulations required that the evaluation contract be awarded
through competitive bidding. It was through this procedure that The Urban
Institute was selected.

The Institute recognized at the outset, as it wrote to the New York
City Police Department in February 1971, that it might be "extremely difficult to tell whether any observed improvement will be due to the special
quality of personnel in the project or to the basic design of the neighborhood
team policing program." This referred to the method of selecting the team
commanders and team members.

One role of the Institute was to make continuing recommendations for the improvement of the neighborhood policing programs. But in order to have an adequate basis for evaluating success, Institute researchers stated that it would be necessary to develop an _experiment_ with a random choice of personnel, a random selection of matched areas, and the collection of extensive baseline data and continuing data.

## PROGRAM EXPANSION

Unfortunately for the evaluation, Operation Neighborhood began to spread like wildfire even before the studies or experiment could be launched. The evaluation was prepared with the belief that there would be from four to nine teams. Actually, the program mushroomed rapidly to cover five entire precincts with 29 teams and 33 additional precincts with either one or two teams each. Over 10 percent of the department's patrol officers were members of teams by 1972.

This growth has not been a model of orderly planning. The police department's coordinating staff, during most of this growth, consisted of two individuals in the office of the director of planning. These individuals had all they could do just to arrange for the opening up of new precincts and the briefing of the new team commanders. There was little or no time to brief precinct commanders, and extremely little time to attend to the problems which team commanders identified in their monthly reports. No patrolmen received special training.

The reasons for this rapid growth are not obscure. The commissioner found that aroused citizen groups often would accept the installation of a new neighborhood police team as a resolution of their problem—at least for the time being. Politically active citizens liked the idea that they would have a team designated for their neighborhood and apparently were reassured by being able to see police cars labelled "Neighborhood Police Team."

## KEY OPERATIONAL PROBLEMS

### INEFFECTIVE IMPLEMENTATION

The complex problems associated with installing effective teams were, for the most part, deferred. Precinct commanders often had an incomplete notion of what team policing involved. Sometimes there were conflicts between team commanders, team patrolmen, and other precinct officials. These conflicts resulted from command conflicts built into the program (the use of sergeants as team commanders and of other sergeants as shift supervisors and lieutenants as operations officers or shift commanders) and from a lack of understanding of the principles of the new program. For example, a team patrolman might be directed by his team commander to patrol a special beat, only to be stopped by a precinct sergeant for departing from a department-authorized beat. Similarly, a team commander might carefully schedule his manpower to be able to have more men available on a particular shift; and the lieutenant in charge of that shift might then take this carefully pre-served manpower away from the team area and assign it to another part of the precinct.

### FAILURE TO IMPLEMENT DISPATCH GUIDELINES

Under dispatch guidelines worked out in the original order, cars were to be sent out of neighborhood team areas only on emergency calls, and then only when other cars were not available. Throughout the entire period of this experiment, the communications division failed to follow these guide-lines. This failure (indicated by analysis of computer tapes furnished by the department) shows up on all shifts and days of the week, regardless of the number of service calls. The failure deprived the operation of two important elements:

- to have patrolmen who are familiar with an area provide service to that area's residents

- to make it more likely that a car will be in the team's area when an emergency run is assigned.

CONFLICTING PROGRAMS

Operation Neighborhood was not installed as an integrated concept, in part, because the department was trying to implement a number of programs simultaneously. For example, a "Career Paths" program, which is antithetical to the concept of neighborhood team policing, was installed at the same time as the team program. In the Career Paths program, officers are rotated regularly among precincts, making it less likely that they would develop meaningful neighborhood ties and more likely that teams would be disrupted through high personnel turnover.

RECENT EFFORTS TO IMPROVE IMPLEMENTATION

There are signs that the police department has decided to make an intensive effort to get Operation Neighborhood accepted by all of the necessary members of the department. As The Urban Institute had recommended in a preliminary report, the chief of patrol organized a nine-member staff to coordinate Operation Neighborhood. He met with borough commanders and division commanders to stress the importance of the program. A training program for Operation Neighborhood is now fully underway, and plans are being made to include precinct commanders in part of the training.

THE TASK AHEAD. The difficulty of winning acceptance for Operation Neighborhood should not be underrated. All elements of the department must be briefed, trained, and encouraged to cooperate. Consideration should be given to organizing task forces of officers and officials to participate in planning for effective implementation in a given division. Until the department makes careful plans to implement the concept, it will not be able to determine its potential.

## EVALUATION PROBLEMS

In its proposal of February 16, 1971, The Urban Institute stated:

> It is important that part of the evaluation contract for Neighborhood Team Policing during the period April 1, 1971 through January 1, 1972 should include extensive research and preparation for a controlled experiment that will be able to answer the ultimate questions about Neighborhood Police Teams. Unless this task is included within the evaluation planned for the earlier period, it will be impossible to get meaningful measurements without delaying for a substantial additional period in order to plan for an experiment.

The proposal contemplated an evaluation which would begin in April, but the evaluation contract was not approved by the Board of Estimate of New York City until the middle of September. Meanwhile, some of the operational considerations within the New York City Police Department had changed. For example, for what are believed to be sound reasons, the New York City Police Department decided not to set up an experiment to test the advantages of Operation Neighborhood. Several factors contributed to this unwillingness:

- unwillingness to accept the administrative constraints needed to conduct an experiment

- a belief by some police officials that Operation Neighborhood is superior to other modes of operation and that it is therefore not justifiable to undertake substantial costs to test this belief further

- desire to meet citizen demands for Operation Neighborhood and not to maintain control groups merely because an evaluation design required them

● political problems with the Board of Estimate if the police department desired to spend additional evaluation money using out-of-town consultants such as The Urban Institute.

Early in the planning for this evaluation, The Urban Institute made it clear that an evaluation which was not designed as an experiment would lack precision in its findings. We presented the arguments for experimentation and the administrative constraints that would have been required for experimentation to proceed. Our answer came from Chief of Patrol Donald Cawley, who used police sources to conclude that Operation Neighborhood merited expansion (it now consists of about 10 percent of the patrol force) and that an experimental evaluation of its relative merit was not called for.

It seems that this was a reasonable decision, made in the best interest of the New York City Police Department. Only when an administrator is unsure of the merits of a program or is considering two competing programs which he believes to have roughly equal merit is a comparative evaluation worth doing.

On the other hand, other police administrators in this nation have different assessments of the potential of Operation Neighborhood or other team policing programs. A substantial segment of those administrators may be interested in a systematic evaluation of Operation Neighborhood--particularly if the evaluation were to take place in more than one city. Unfortunately, these administrators do not have the power to make New York City act in their interest rather than solely in its own interest.

The federal government seems to be the only institution that can represent this national need to know. If it chooses to act to foster local experimentation, a local jurisdication may produce knowledge useful throughout the nation. Because experimentation may involve local costs--both administrative and monetary--it is appropriate that the federal government provide an adequate subsidy to encourage a jurisdiction to accept these costs.

New York City and many other cities might be willing to participate in a program of controlled experimentation providing that:

- cities are subsidized to cover their costs

- the experiments planned in different cities all will have the potential of producing useful operational knowledge.

At present, police or criminal justice experimentation (with experimental treatments and comparison areas) is rare in this nation. Federal agencies might, therefore, review their priorities and use a substantial portion of the available research and action funds to encourage the kind of activity which will produce both knowledge and action. At present, the federal government is buying some action but little knowledge.

SUMMARY OF EVALUATION PROBLEMS

This evaluation has been an effort to catch on to a program that has been taking off like a jet. The impressions often are subjective. The evaluation lacks the precision which might have been possible had the police department undertaken a controlled experiment of its important innovation.

Since New York did not conduct an experiment, this evaluation has had to rely on: (1) observations, inquiries, and judgments of the evaluators, (2) available data which often have been ambiguous both because of how they were collected and because of the lack of adequate comparison groups to use as baselines, and (3) some limited surveys of police and citizens. All of this information is "management information." Although comparison precincts were selected, they are only roughly similar to experimental precincts and to volunteer neighborhood police teams. Therefore, data interpretation is more artful than scientific. Its usefulness is improved if one has a thorough knowledge of the police institution to which it relates.

It is hoped that, despite the difficulties involved in doing this kind of evaluation, the study provides useful insights into operational problems and potential advantages of Operation Neighborhood. It is intended to help police administrators understand the concept and decide whether to use it.


CONCLUSIONS AND RECOMMENDATIONS

Operation Neighborhood apparently has led to a modest improvement in crime reduction and to more arrests by patrolmen. In general, this result has been produced without creating any basic changes in police job satisfaction or patrol attitudes. Looking at the variety of measures used in this report, one can infer that team members may be motivated to do more, but that the way they perform is very much the same as before they joined Operation Neighborhood.

Operation Neighborhood has an excellent public relations image and has won a measure of popular acceptance. People seem to expect that Operation Neighborhood, if continued, will have a greater beneficial effect in the future.

The program is not without its important defects. For example, the communications division has not yet implemented guidelines designed to permit teams to service the neighborhood in which they may have become expert. The Career Paths program often rotates team patrolmen who have become familiar with a neighborhood. Precinct commanders and other precinct officials may fail to understand the program or may even resist its implementation (as occurred in the training program). Some teams may be creating potential resistance in the community by using aggressive patrol tactics such as stop-and-frisk.  Teams apparently are not placing greater emphasis on investigation and the use of information gained from citizens.

## PROGRESS ON MAJOR OBJECTIVES OF
## OPERATION NEIGHBORHOOD

Because the police department has not clearly communicated a high priority for Operation Neighborhood, the program has not been fully implemented nor fairly tested.  Nevertheless, it is appropriate to look at the objectives of Operation Neighborhood and to determine the extent to which they have been achieved.

### CONTROLLING CRIME

Operation Neighborhood has reported a somewhat larger reduction in crime than the rest of the department.  The difference is small, a 13 percent reduction compared to 10 percent in the rest of the department.  (This apparent advantage of Operation Neighborhood could be due to random variation in crime statistics or to factors other than police activities.)

### INCREASING COMMUNITY COOPERATION IN
### CRIME CONTROL

Overall, there has been no significant improvement in developing community cooperation.  Yet some team commanders have taken impressive steps to involve the community.  For example, one team commander actively uses community meetings to disseminate information about criminals believed to be active in the area.  He also gathers information from citizens about criminal activity at these meetings.  While some team commanders may be increasing the use of investigative activities, this has not been true programwide.

The teams need to increase community cooperation and, at the same time, develop effective methods of using the information that they gain. Overall, there is little indication that information currently being obtained is being put to good use.

IMPROVING POLICE-COMMUNITY RELATIONS

Some politically active groups have sought the program and supported it in their neighborhoods. The principal support in the area surveyed, however, came from business people. There is no measurable reduction in people's fear of crime nor improvement in their general attitudes toward police that can be attributed to the program.

AVOIDING VIOLENCE. One interesting incident reveals the potential of Operation Neighborhood for avoiding violence (an effect which is difficult to measure directly). For example, one Brooklyn precinct commander reports that a team in his precinct held a meeting with local Black Muslims. Subsequently, tactical police units became involved in an incident in front of their mosque. The tactical police were attempting to arrest a man who was driving without headlights at night. Men inside the mosque were angry at the treatment being given to their "brother" and they were leaning out of the windows making threatening remarks. At that point, two team policemen arrived. They introduced themselves to two of the men whom they had previously met and managed to control the situation, with the result that the tactical police left the scene. The next day the minister from the mosque thanked the precinct commander for averting bloodshed.

This incident highlights the importance of even small, unmeasurable improvements in police-community relations. It also illustrates the danger of treating policemen as interchangeable units that can be dispatched mechanically instead of developing dispatch guidelines to assure that informed local police will be sent on calls requiring intimate knowledge of local situations.

AGGRESSIVE TACTICS.  The patrol survey[2] indicates that some teams are engaging in aggressive patrol tactics, such as stop-and-frisk, that may generate citizen antagonism in the long-run.

In one precinct where written communications were studied, written complaints decreased and written commendations of police increased.  Aggressive patrol policies, however, could counteract these short-term beneficial effects on community relations.

TAILORING POLICE OPERATIONS TO THE
NEEDS OF LOCAL COMMUNITIES

Some team commanders report the initiation of programs that have won local acceptance.  For example, apartment building security surveys, during which residents are informed of ways to protect their lives and property, are quite popular.  Also well received in the neighborhoods is the use of volunteers.  These civilian police auxiliaries help maintain order at special events, walk foot-beats when regular police are not available, and assist as translators in patrol cars serving Spanish-speaking areas.

Such programs, of course, could have been implemented without Operation Neighborhood.  Clear evidence is not yet available to ascertain whether programs catering to local needs are more likely to be implemented by team commanders than by precinct commanders.

In the course of this project, reports from team commanders have been reviewed and--like the command officials in the police department--the evaluators have been impressed by the dedication and resourcefulness of department personnel.  For example, in an analysis of team commander reports

---

2.  See Evaluation Design, p. 21.

for the month of March, the evaluators stated:

> Analysis of the March team commander reports shows that
> Operation Neighborhood appears to be making positive strides toward
> meeting its stated objectives.  Of the many special programs men-
> tioned, many deal with breaking down barriers which exist between
> students and police through honest communication.  There has been
> an increase in the number of teams making large numbers of public
> contacts and a continued use of auxiliary police and civilians.

It is obvious that, in a program as large as Operation Neighborhood,
there are some teams that are exceptionally good or exceptionally bad.
Because of limited resources, the evaluators have had to concentrate on a
few teams and on overall program statistics.  As the department already
knows, there are some commanders who have become very popular within their
neighborhoods, others who seem to have had an important effect on crime, and
still others who have gotten nowhere.  When asked about the program, some
officers say that it does not affect what they do on their job.  Other
officers, however, are very loyal to their commanders and to the team program.

At this point, the successes of individual commanders have not trans-
lated themselves into statistics which reflect favorably on the overall
program.

INCREASING POLICE OFFICER JOB SATISFACTION

Major improvements in police job satisfaction and basic job attitudes
have not been detected among police assigned to teams.  Team members do
register somewhat less dissatisfaction with pay and hours, compared to others
on the police force.  Also, as indicated in our quarterly report,[3] neighborhood police team "volunteers" use about half the sick leave of other officers
in the same precincts (.62 days in three months compared to 1.28 days in
three months).  But this is outweighed by the negative finding that 80 percent of team members believe their job is getting worse rather than better.

_____

3.    Peter B. Bloch and David I. Specht, Quarterly Report on Operation
Neighborhood (1972), The Urban Institute.

## IMPROVING THE WORKING RELATIONSHIP BETWEEN
## OFFICERS AND THEIR IMMEDIATE SUPERVISORS

Neighborhood team members are more likely to talk regularly to a sergeant about their job problems. Since a sergeant is assigned to each team, this was expected. Surprisingly, little further evidence of an improved supervisory relationship was uncovered. On the contrary, team patrolmen do not offer more suggestions to their supervisors, they do not believe their supervisors are significantly more understanding, and they do not believe their own job performance is better known to their supervisors.

## INCREASING POLICE EFFICIENCY

Arrests and summonses per man are somewhat higher for team members than for the rest of the police department. Arrest statistics may be misleading because information about the "soundness" of arrests or the disposition of arrests in the courts is not available.

Team members answer their fair share of radio runs. In some teams, they perform additional tasks such as making community-relations contacts. Beyond the inconclusive statistics on arrests and summonses, there is no quantitative evidence of increased efficiency due to Operation Neighborhood.

## RECOMMENDATIONS

On balance, Operation Neighborhood appears to have had some success despite the conflicting demands which resulted in less than total commitment from department leadership. Results are sufficiently promising to merit controlled expansion. However, greater command effort is called for if the program, as initially designed, is to receive a full and fair test.

The police commissioner, the chief inspector, and the chief of patrol should inform all concerned officials that implementation of Operation

Neighborhood is mandatory. Borough, division, and precinct commanders should be required to exercise their authority to support this important program. This includes developing leadership methods to coordinate support for neighborhood teams, rather than permitting command jealousies to interfere with operations.

The New York City Police Department should consider testing the neighborhood team policing ideas being developed by Cincinnati. Among these are the use of lieutenants instead of sergeants as team commanders and assigning detectives to teams, in part to instruct other team members in investigative techniques.

Dispatch procedures should be modified to reduce out-of-sector assignments. Those responsible for the Operation Neighborhood training program should develop means to give trainers greater access to the officers they are supposed to train.

People at all levels of the operational planning process should be directed to conform their plans to the Operation Neighborhood concept. For example, Operation Neighborhood encourages police-civilian contacts. Nevertheless, recent orders were issued to ban patrolmen from talking with shopkeepers or shopping in local stores. This created resentment among police officers and disrupted the operation of some teams.

Assignments of newly hired and trained police officers should not be concentrated in just a few precincts where a high turnover could destroy rapport between neighborhood teams and the community.

The minority recruitment program should be geared to bring in candidates who could serve in Operation Neighborhood. Black officers have obvious advantages in establishing closer cooperation with black communities.

In developing incentives to achieve higher professionalism among police, the reward system for patrolmen should be improved. In the current reward system, too much emphasis is placed on numbers of arrests, without regard for the soundness of the arrests. More recognition should be given to officers who are good at settling fights, conducting community relations campaigns or collecting information from the community--all skills important to good neighborhood teams.

The police department, directly or through an outside agency, should continue evaluation activities similar to those undertaken for this report. This will assist the department in implementing recommendations for program improvement and in evaluating their effects. Such evaluations will provide operating personnel with feedback on whether the program is performing as intended, whether activities developed by precinct or team commanders merit study or dissemination, and whether particular problems require resolution. Ultimately, an evaluation capability will permit the department to decide whether Operation Neighborhood--in its current or modified form--should be continued.

II

EVALUATION DESIGN

Three principal types of measurements were used in this evaluation--a patrol survey, citizen survey, and department measures. Table 2 shows how experimental groups (where team policing is used) were compared to some related comparison groups. In each instance, the comparison is rough. This is typical of evaluations for programs set up as pilot projects rather than as experiments.

PATROL SURVEY METHODOLOGY

The patrol survey was designed by The Urban Institute in consultation with Captain John Watters, then coordinator of Operation Neighborhood, Sergeant Anthony Vastolla, assistant to Captain Watters, and Captain Frank Mendyk, Jr., of the chief of patrol's office.

Questionnaires were distributed to patrolmen in experimental and comparison groups during the months of January, April, and June 1972. Table 3 shows the number of questionnaires used in the evaluation.

The experimental groups which were surveyed include: (1) Volunteers, (2) Precinct 34, (3) Precinct 6, and (4) Precinct 24. Table 4, "Neighborhood Police Teams in Sample," indicates the dates on which each of the experimental groups began operating under Operation Neighborhood. Because of operational changes in the program, Precincts 14 and 24 were included in the sample of volunteer teams during the January survey but were replaced with similar precincts (Precincts 17 and 25) during subsequent waves of interviewing.

TABLE 2: EVALUATION DESIGN

| Measurement Instruments | Purpose | Operation Neighborhood Groups | Related Comparison Groups |
|---|---|---|---|
| Patrol Survey | (1) Attitudes of patrolmen: toward community, toward supervisors, toward their job<br><br>(2) Observations of patrolmen about community attitudes | (1) 34th Precinct<br><br>(2) Volunteers (sample of seven NPTs in different precincts)<br><br>(3) 24th Precinct<br><br>(4) 6th Precinct Volunteers | (1) 114th Precinct<br><br>(2) Comparisons (sample of officers from same precinct as volunteers)<br><br>(3) 114th Precinct 79th Precinct<br><br>(4) No direct comparison groups; the team was chosen because it was believed superior to most other teams. It should be compared to all the comparison groups and the department |
| Citizen Survey | (1) Measure citizen recognition<br><br>(2) Determine impact on citizens | (1) 34th Precinct | (1) 114th Precinct |
| Department Measures | (1) Arrest productivity<br>(2) Effect on crime rates<br>(3) Citizen complaints<br>(4) Absenteeism<br>(5) Records of dispatching NPT cars | (1) Same groups as patrol survey plus, where available, statistics for all neighborhood teams | (1) Same groups as patrol survey, plus department-wide statistics |

# TABLE 3: NUMBER OF QUESTIONNAIRES USED IN THE EVALUATION

## OPERATION NEIGHBORHOOD GROUPS

| SURVEY WAVE | VOLUNTEERS Percent Returned | Percent on Patrol and with Seniority* Information | Number Used | PRECINCT 34 Percent Returned | Percent on Patrol and with Seniority Information | Number Used | PRECINCT 6 Percent Returned | Percent on Patrol and with Seniority Information | Number Used | PRECINCT 24 Percent Returned | Percent on Patrol and with Seniority Information | Number Used |
|---|---|---|---|---|---|---|---|---|---|---|---|---|
| January | 57 | 57 | 16 | 90 | 80 | 24 | -- | -- | -- | -- | -- | -- |
| April | 89 | 79 | 22 | 70 | 57 | 17 | -- | -- | -- | -- | -- | -- |
| June | 71 | 61 | 17 | 57 | 50 | 15 | 60 | 60 | 18 | 63 | 47 | 14 |
| TOTAL | 71 | 65 | 55 | 74 | 62 | 56 | 60 | 60 | 18 | 63 | 47 | 14 |

## COMPARISON GROUPS

| SURVEY WAVE | COMPARISONS Percent Returned | Percent on Patrol and with Seniority Information | Number Used | PRECINCT 114 Percent Returned | Percent on Patrol and with Seniority Information | Number Used | PRECINCT 79 Percent Returned | Percent on Patrol and with Seniority Information | Number Used |
|---|---|---|---|---|---|---|---|---|---|
| January | 61 | 61 | 17 | 87 | 53 | 8 | -- | -- | -- |
| April | 89 | 79 | 22 | 57 | 50 | 15 | 57 | 40 | 12 |
| June | 54 | 46 | 13 | 43 | 40 | 12 | 43 | 33 | 10 |
| TOTAL | 68 | 49 | 52 | 57 | 47 | 35 | 51 | 33 | 22 |

*Since a patrolman's seniority was essential for our analysis, we used only questionnaires disclosing seniority. Since some officers indicated that they had not patrolled at all in the last month, we decided that their questionnaires also should not be used in the analysis.

TABLE 4: NEIGHBORHOOD POLICE TEAMS IN SAMPLE

| Neighborhood Police Teams * | Date of Implementation | Survey Dates |
|---|---|---|
| 6 (specially selected) | 6-03-71 | June only |
| 14 (volunteer) | 12-07-71 | January only |
| 17 (volunteer) | 2-23-72 | April and June |
| 24 | 2-02-72 (volunteer team) | January only |
| | 6-25-71 (precinct-wide) six teams | June only |
| 25 (volunteer) | 7-16-71 | April and June |
| 34 (five teams) | 8-17-71 | January, April, June |
| 44 (volunteer) | 7-29-71 | January, April, June |
| 60 (volunteer) | 4-29-71 | January, April, June |
| 71 (volunteer) | 2-25-71 | January, April, June |
| 94 (volunteer) | 10-05-71 | January, April, June |
| 109 (volunteer) | 2-11-71 | January, April, June |

*Numbers in this column indicate the precincts which contain Neighborhood Police Teams.

Comparison groups consist of (1) comparisons (non-volunteers from the same precincts as volunteer teams), (2) Precinct 114 (a comparison precinct) and (3) Precinct 79 (a comparison precinct). Table 5 shows the average seniority of patrolmen interviewed in June for each of the sample groups used in the study. Note that men in most neighborhood teams are somewhat younger than those in comparison groups.

Precinct 114 was selected as a comparison group on the basis of conferences with Captain John Watters and Captain Frank Mendyk, Jr. The match is less than perfect, both because 114th Precinct patrolmen have greater seniority (see Table 5) and because the 114th Precinct has a lower crime rate than does the 34th Precinct (see Table 6).

To help the reader better interpret the data, Precinct 79 was selected as a second comparison precinct. Tables 6, 7, and 8 show the 1971 crime rates, 1970 ethnic distribution and 1968 income distribution for Precinct 34 and the two comparison precincts. Note that the racial composition of Precinct 34 is similar to that of Precinct 114. Precinct 79, located in Brooklyn, is 75 percent black and 15 percent Puerto Rican--a much greater minority representation than in Precincts 34 or 114.

## SUBJECT AREAS ON THE PATROL SURVEY

Table 9 gives a brief presentation of the subject areas which were of concern to us in the patrol survey. Subsequent sections of this report discuss each subject area in greater depth, giving the reasons why team policing might have caused changes in particular subject areas and discussing the changes which were actually found.

TABLE 5:   AVERAGE SENIORITY OF PATROLMEN INTERVIEWED
IN JUNE--FOR ALL SAMPLE GROUPS

| GROUP | AVERAGE SENIORITY (In Years) |
|---|---|
| Precinct 34 | 7.88 |
| Precinct 24 | 6.44 |
| Precinct 6 | 6.06 |
| Volunteers | 6.34 |
| All Operation Neighborhood Groups* | 6.82 |
| Precinct 114 | 12.23 |
| Precinct 79 | 7.85 |
| Comparisons (non-volunteers within same precincts as volunteers) | 7.21 |
| All Comparison Groups** | 9.05 |

*Precincts 34, 24, 6, and Volunteers

**Precincts 114, 79, and Comparisons

TABLE 6: 1971 REPORTED CRIME AND CRIME RATE/100,000 PERSONS, F.B.I. INDEX

| Crime Category | 34TH PRECINCT | | 114TH PRECINCT | | 79TH PRECINCT | |
|---|---|---|---|---|---|---|
| | No. of Crimes | Rate/100,000 | No. of Crimes | Rate/100,000 | No. of Crimes | Rate/100,000 |
| Murder | 13 | 9.53 | 13 | 5.82 | 58 | 53.7 |
| Forcible Rape | 33 | 21.65 | 21 | 9.40 | 60 | 55.5 |
| Robbery | 1201 | 787.75 | 766 | 342.85 | 1172 | 1084.3 |
| Aggravated Assault | 355 | 232.85 | 338 | 151.28 | 1009 | 933.5 |
| TOTAL (Violent) | 1602 | 1050.77 | 1138 | 509.35 | 2299 | 2127.0 |
| Burglary | 2845 | 1866.06 | 2392 | 1070.62 | 2749 | 2543.4 |
| Larceny $50 | 1329 | 871.70 | 1558 | 697.34 | 1223 | 1131.5 |
| Auto Theft | 1030 | 675.59 | 3282 | 1468.98 | 661 | 611.6 |
| TOTAL (Property) | 5204 | 3413.35 | 7232 | 3236.94 | 4633 | 4286.5 |
| TOTAL (Index) | 6806 | 4464.12 | 8370 | 3746.29 | 6932 | 6413.5 |

1970 Population--U.S. Census

| | |
|---|---|
| 34th Precinct | 152,460 |
| 114th Precinct | 223,421 |
| 79th Precinct | 108,000 |

TABLE 7:  ESTIMATED 1970 ETHNIC DISTRIBUTION*
(BY PRECINCT)

| Demographic Group | 34th | 114th | 79th |
|---|---|---|---|
| White | 70% | 80% | 10% |
| Black | 10% | 15% | 75% |
| Puerto Rican | 20% | 5% | 15% |

TABLE 8:  ESTIMATED 1968 INCOME DISTRIBUTION* (ALL HOUSEHOLDS)
(BY PRECINCT)

| Income | 34th | 114th | 79th |
|---|---|---|---|
| Less than $2,000 | 14% | 11% | 21% |
| $2,000 - $2,999 | 8% | 5% | 12% |
| $3,000 - $5,999 | 34% | 32% | 42% |
| $6,000 - $9,999 | 30% | 33% | 19% |
| $10,000 - $14,999 | 10% | 15% | 4% |
| $15,000 and over | 4% | 4% | 1% |

*All estimates made from the New York City Master Plan, Planning
District data.

TABLE 9: SUBJECT AREAS IN THE PATROL SURVEY

| SUBJECT AREAS | SUBJECTS |
|---|---|
| Supervision | Regular contact with a sergeant. Superiors' knowledge about officers' job performance. Authoritarian beliefs. |
| Extrinsic Job Satisfaction | Pay<br>Hours |
| Citizen Cooperation | Cooperation in providing crime information. Willingness to report crime. Number of cooperating citizens or informants. |
| Citizen Support | Appreciation by the public. Willingness of citizens to tell truth to help wrongfully accused police officer. Willingness to help a police officer in trouble. Percentage of people supporting police. Number of compliments from citizens. |
| Attitude Toward Community | Importance of breaking up groups of loiterers. Importance of harassing criminals on weak charges. Effectiveness of "aggressive patrol." Importance of preventive patrol. Importance of preliminary investigation. Importance of talking to citizens. Importance of foot patrol. |
| Corruption | Availability of a tip or meal. |
| Citizen Hostility | Threatened or attempted injury. Bystanders wishing police officers to be harmed. Membership in groups opposed to police. General bystander hostility. Danger of policing. |
| Satisfaction with Policing Tasks | Frequency of job satisfaction. Interest of the job. Sense of accomplishment. Belief in need to use discretion. Potential effectiveness against narcotics. Usefulness to the public. Rating job activities as important rather than as not important. |
| Vehicle Dispatch | Distance traveled per dispatch. |
| Index of Change | Change in willingness of citizens to report burglaries. Change in willingness of citizens to be complaining witnesses. |

## MATHEMATICAL ANALYSIS OF THE PATROL SURVEY

To measure differences between Operation Neighborhood groups and comparison groups, the patrol survey was administered (see Appendix B). To determine whether expected results had occurred, groups of questions were combined into **indexes**. One index was constructed for each area of interest shown in Table 9. (See Appendix C for the **formula used**.) In addition to analyzing these **indexes**, the individual questions were analyzed separately in light of the purposes of the neighborhood team policing program.

A simultaneous linear regression technique was used for the analysis. The computation was accomplished through the use of a computer program package called "ICARUS." The package was developed by George Sadowsky of The Urban Institute and Kenneth Jacobs of The Brookings Institution.

A sample regression equation (initial form) is presented in Table 10. Notice that each of the experimental groups is an independent variable in the equation. Furthermore, a time variable was included for each group whenever a survey was taken at more than one point in time. In the sample equation, "log of seniority" is used as an independent variable. Because of the difficulty of determining on an a priori basis what form of the seniority variable is most likely to explain differences in a dependent variable, we used the natural log of seniority (in years) and two other forms of the variable. The first was a linear form. The second, a dichotomous or dummy variable form, was equal to zero whenever seniority was three years or less, and equal to one whenever seniority was greater than three years. In addition to the time variables for each group, note that a separate time variable was included for each of the waves in order to test the assumption that there was an overall change from one wave to another.

TABLE 10: SAMPLE REGRESSION EQUATION (INITIAL FORM)

| Dependent Variable | Independent Variables and Constant | Definition of Previously Undefined Variables |
|---|---|---|
| Number of insults = | $a_1$ + | Constant Term |
| | $a_2$ x Precinct 34 + | $a_2$ = Coefficient of this term. Precinct 34 = Dummy variable (= 1 for members of Precinct 34, and otherwise = 0) |
| | $a_3$ x $T_1$ x Precinct 34 + | $T_1$ = Dummy variable equal to one for observations taken in January |
| | $a_4$ x $T_2$ x Precinct 34 + | $T_2$ = Dummy variable equal to one for observations taken in April |
| | $a_5$ x Precinct 24 + | |
| | $a_6$ x Precinct 6 + | |
| | $a_7$ x volunteers + | |
| | $a_8$ x $T_1$ x volunteers + | |
| | $a_9$ x $T_2$ x volunteers + | |
| | $a_{10}$ x Precinct 114 + | |
| | $a_{11}$ x $T_1$ Precinct 114 + | |
| | $a_{12}$ x $T_2$ Precinct 114 + | |
| | $a_{13}$ x Precinct 79 + | |
| | $a_{14}$ x $T_2$ x Precinct 79 + | |
| | $a_{15}$ x log of seniority | |
| | $a_{16}$ x $T_1$ | |
| | $a_{17}$ x $T_2$ | |

After the initial form of the regression was run, t-tests were per-
formed on each of the regression coefficients. First, the form of the
seniority variable with the highest $t$ was determined. That form would be
used in follow-up regressions. Next, each of the time variables was examined to determine whether the $t$ value was significant at the .1 level
(for 250 degrees of freedom). If the $t$ value was significant, then the time
trend variables were used in the follow-up regression equation. If the
value was not significant, or if the $t$ value was significant in the initial
form of the regression equation, but was not significant in subsequent forms,
then the time variables were dropped and the data for the different waves
were combined.

For example, if the coefficients $a_3$ or $a_4$ (see Table 10) were significant in the sample regression equation, then the time interactions would be
retained for Precinct 34 in the second run. If none of the coefficients
$a_8$, $a_9$, $a_{14}$, $a_{16}$ or $a_{17}$ was significant, then all would be dropped from the
second run. Assuming that the $t$ value for the log of seniority was higher
than the $t$ value for the other forms of seniority, then the following run
would be made for this dependent variable (see Table 11):

TABLE 11: SAMPLE REGRESSION EQUATION (SECOND RUN)

Number of insults = $b_1 + b_2$ x Precinct 34 + $b_3$ x $T_1$ x Precinct 34
+ $b_4$ x $T_2$ x Precinct 34 + $b_5$ x Precinct 24
+ $b_6$ x Precinct 6 + $b_7$ x volunteers
+ $b_8$ x log of seniority

Note that there has not been much concern for the significance of the equation in determining the dependent variable. The $\underline{F}$ value, the $R^2$ or corrected $R^2$ values were not utilized.

Different forms of the equations were tried to determine whether the experimental groups were different from one or more of the comparison groups. A difference was reported as significant if the $\underline{t}$ value was significant at the .1 level or better on a two-tailed test. That is, a difference was reported as significant if there was one chance in ten that the difference could have occurred by chance.

In addition to presenting the significant results, tables of "expected values" are presented to enable the reader to see the magnitude of the differences which were isolated through the use of the statistical technique. On occasion, raw tabulations of our data are also presented for further comparison by the reader. Table 12 shows the way in which a sample of expected values is computed. The reader should bear in mind that, unless tables are labelled "raw data," the values being presented were computed in the manner presented in this table.

TABLE 12:   COMPUTATION OF SAMPLE EXPECTED VALUES (FROM TABLE 11)

All Comparison Groups Combined = $b_1$ (omitting an adjustment for log of seniority*)

Precinct 24 = $b_1 + b_5$ (omitting an adjustment for log of seniority)

Precinct 34 in June ($T_3$, the omitted time term) = $b_1 + b_2$ (omitting an adjustment for log of seniority)

Precinct 34 in January ($T_1$) = $b_1 + b_2 + b_3$ (omitting an adjustment for log of seniority)

*To find the expected value for an individual, find the expected value for his group and add the natural log of his seniority, in years. To readjust the expected value for a group, add the log of the average seniority of that group. However, the adjustment process will reinstate seniority differences, giving less meaning to comparisons among groups.

## THE COMMUNITY SURVEY

Community survey respondents were chosen from among: residents, businessmen, participants in community groups, and high school students. The survey attempted to compare citizens in the 34th Precinct, where Operation Neighborhood has been implemented in all sectors, to citizens in the 114th Precinct, where there are no neighborhood teams.

Residents were selected in the following manner. First, one residential block was selected from each of the five team areas in the 34th Precinct. Residents within these blocks were then selected with equal probability using systematic random sampling from a reverse telephone directory. A single block was then selected in the 114th Precinct. Since all resident interviews were conducted by telephone, only individuals with listed telephones were included in the sample. An introductory letter was mailed prior to contact.

Businessmen in both precincts were selected, first, by choosing streets known to have heavy concentration of businesses. Individual business establishments were then selected at random from a reverse telephone directory. Interviews were conducted in person at the place of business. The manager or owner was interviewed in most cases, but any employee was accepted for inter-viewing. All businessmen received an introductory letter before they were contacted for the interview.

The sample of people who had attended community meetings was limited to the 34th Precinct. People were selected from groups that had been addressed by the team commanders. Five community meeting participants were selected from each of the five team areas. In order to make the sample more representative, two of the participants were chosen from Community Council attendance records and the remaining three were selected from three different community organizations (such as tenant groups, church groups, and school parent organizations). All interviews were conducted by telephone.

The school students were from the George Washington High School (34th Precinct) and Brandeis High School (114th Precinct). Selection was from a health education class, and school administrators selected an all female class in George Washington High School and a mixed male-female sample in the Brandeis High School. All students were then screened by the interviewers to make sure they resided within the boundaries of the respective precincts. All student interviews were face-to-face. The sex of the respondents in the two student samples differed but our survey instruments do not indicate the sex of the respondent.

Table 13 gives the number of interviews analyzed in each group in the sample.

TABLE 13:   NUMBER OF COMMUNITY SURVEY INTERVIEWS ANALYZED

| Group | 34th Precinct | 114th Precinct |
|---|---|---|
| Residents | 30 | 14 |
| Businessmen | 40 | 20 |
| Youth | 30 | 20 |
| Community Meeting Participants | 25 | -- |

Interpretation of results from the community survey should be made with great care. These samples are not truly representative and the sample sizes are too small to give great confidence in the interpretation of results. In addition, the precincts being compared are not strictly comparable.

III

EFFECT ON CRIME AND ARRESTS

Reported crime statistics indicate that police serving in Operation Neighborhood were somewhat more effective than those in the rest of the department in reducing robbery, total violent crimes, total property crimes and total index crimes during the period April through June 1972. This greater effectiveness in dealing with crime appears not to be a result of changes in the crime reporting system.[4]

In addition, Operation Neighborhood police appear to make more arrests per man than police in the rest of the department. It is not known whether the increased arrests are "sound" according to court standards, that is, whether a high ratio of arrests leads to convictions.

CRIME COMPARISONS

Table 14 presents the percentage of change in reported crime for areas served by team police, by their host precincts (including the teams), the all-team precincts, and the comparison precincts for the periods April-June, 1971 and April-June, 1972.

---

4. While the research methods justify at least tentative confidence in these findings, further statistical evidence over time is desirable both to verify the conclusion and to test whether crime reduction may be a permanent feature of team policing. In the absence of more rigorous evaluation, it must be noted that the favorable data could result from random variation, the use of volunteers in the program, to other favorable factors beyond police activities in areas under Operation Neighborhood, or to unfavorable factors in the areas that did not use team policing.

TABLE 14: PERCENTAGE CHANGE OF REPORTED CRIME FOR AREAS SERVED BY NEIGHBORHOOD POLICE TEAMS, HOST PRECINCTS, AND COMPARISON PRECINCTS, FROM APRIL THROUGH JUNE 1971 TO APRIL THROUGH JUNE 1972.

| CRIME CATEGORY | TEAMS[1] AND HOST PRECINCTS[2] | | | | | | | | | | | | ALL-TEAM PRECINCTS | | COMPARISON PRECINCTS | |
| --- | --- | --- | --- | --- | --- | --- | --- | --- | --- | --- | --- | --- | --- | --- | --- | --- |
| | Group I | | Group II | | Group III | | Group IV | | 6th Precinct | | 77th Precinct[3] | | 34th | 24th | 114th | 79th |
| | Team | Precinct | Team | Precinct | Team | Precinct | Team | Precinct | Team | Precinct | Team | Precinct | | | | |
| Robbery | -24.8 | -10.9 | -11.6 | + 6.0 | - .2 | - 2.2 | -14.6 | +39.6 | -26.3 | - 4.4 | -45.8 | +18.9 | +22.3 | -14.3 | +17.0 | +45.6 |
| Total Violent | -16.2 | - 2.3 | - 6.2 | +10.7 | + 5.6 | - 2.5 | - .4 | +45.3 | -37.0 | - 8.9 | -37.0 | +17.2 | +19.3 | - 9.6 | +23.6 | +25.8 |
| Burglary | -11.2 | - 2.6 | - .6 | - 4.7 | - 4.4 | + 2.3 | - .2 | - 5.4 | +33.1 | +18.4 | -18.3 | +19.2 | -41.3 | -17.6 | -15.0 | - 6.7 |
| Total Property | -20.4 | -14.4 | -15.7 | -17.3 | - 8.5 | - 6.7 | -21.0 | - 5.9 | - .9 | -23.8 | -34.4 | + 4.1 | -39.1 | -18.3 | -20.9 | -14.9 |
| Total Index | -19.3 | -11.4 | -13.0 | -10.8 | - 3.7 | - 3.9 | -17.7 | + 3.4 | - 1.0 | -21.1 | -35.1 | + 8.8 | -27.9 | -15.6 | -15.6 | - 1.9 |

1. Group I: Teams implemented January-March 1971 (47th, 109th, 32nd, 120th, 71st).

   Group II: Teams implemented April-June 1971 (6th, 9th, 23rd, 43rd, 45th, 48th, 60th, 68th).

   Group III: Teams implemented July-September 1971 (20th, 25th, 26th, 30th, 44th, 46th, 78th, 103rd, 106th).

   Group IV: Teams implemented October-December 1971 (67th, 69th, 90th, 94th, 105-1, 105-2, 105th (2 teams) ).

2. "Host precinct" refers to the precincts in which the teams are located. The data for host precincts include crimes reported in team areas.

3. "Team" in the 77th Precinct denotes crime data for the first team established in that precinct on January 1, 1971. "Precinct" denotes the remaining five teams established in the rest of the precinct on April 4, 1972. It should also be noted that the 77th was reorganized to include the 80th Precinct on this date and the data for the precinct are based on estimates of 1971 crime for the larger area.

Source: All precinct data were obtained from the FBI Index (except in the 77th Precinct) and all team data were obtained from team commanders quarterly reports, which rely on precinct records and use New York State crime classifications.

Overall, the teams had a greater decrease in reported crime than their host precincts. The reported crime figures for the teams were compiled from precinct records and are based on the New York State Criminal Code, whereas precinct data are based on the FBI Crime Index. While these two codes differ in their definitions of some crimes, definitions for robbery and burglary closely parallel each other. However, the FBI Crime Index defines a theft as a grand larceny if the value of the stolen item is $50 or more, whereas the State Code defines a theft as grand larceny if the value of the item is $200 or more, of if the theft is from a person. Thus, in the 24th Precinct for the three-month period April through June, grand larceny decreased 11.2 percent (using the FBI Index) and increased 36.6 percent (using the New York State Criminal Code). It would be useful if future data collected by the department and used to evaluate the neighborhood team program (or any department program) were standardized to allow more meaningful comparisons.

Data for all neighborhood teams combined indicate a reduction in robbery (-.4 percent), total violent crimes (-.3 percent), total property crimes (-21.1 percent), and total index crime (-13.4 percent). These figures were appreciably better than the citywide figures for the same period. (See Table 15.) This performance of Operation Neighborhood appears substantially better than in the period of September through December 1971 when the teams had a better record for robbery and total violent crimes than did police citywide but a poorer record for other crime categories.[5]

Volunteer teams were examined according to their dates of implementation to find out whether those that had been in operation longer might show greater success in reducing reported crime. (See Note 1, Table 14.) Although the trend is not consistent over the four groups, Group I (the first group of teams to be implemented) did reveal greater reductions in

5.   Bloch and Specht, op. cit. p. 3.

TABLE 15:  PERCENTAGE CHANGE OF CRIMES IN NEIGHBORHOOD
TEAM AREAS COMPARED WITH ENTIRE CITY

| CRIMES | GROUPS | April–June 1971 | April–June 1972 | Percent Change |
|--------|--------|-----------------|-----------------|----------------|
| Robbery | All Team Areas<br>Citywide | 3,088<br>19,183 | 2,968<br>19,580 | − .4<br>+ 2.1 |
| Total<br>Violent | All Team Areas<br>Citywide | 4,088<br>29,003 | 3,965<br>30,387 | − .3<br>+ 4.8 |
| Total<br>Property | All Team Areas<br>Citywide | 9,698<br>96,896 | 7,654<br>82,480 | −21.1<br>−14.9 |
| Total<br>Index | All Team Areas<br>Citywide | 13,786<br>125,899 | 11,940<br>112,867 | −13.4<br>−10.4 |

Source:  Team statistics come from team commander quarterly reports.  Citywide statistics are compiled by the department for the FBI Uniform Crime
Reports.

crime than all other groups and in all categories except one (total property crime for Group IV was down 21.0 percent compared to 20.4 percent for Group I). The crime reduction record was good for Groups I, II, IV, and the all-team precincts (34th and 24th). The 114th Precinct, used for comparison purposes, also showed a substantial reduction in crime.

## CRIME REPORTING PRACTICES

During the time of this study, no effort was made by the department to alter crime statistics in team areas simply by changing reporting practices. Team commanders were made responsible for reducing crime, but this same responsibility was assigned to precinct commanders. Thus, any incentive to change crime reporting practices should have affected precinct and team commanders equally. (The incentive for precinct commanders was so strong that the department was required to take disciplinary action against several precinct commanders who were found to have been rigging their statistics.)

No formal method was developed at the outset for comparing Operation Neighborhood statistics to precinct statistics, so it is not impossible that team commanders could have affected the way their men reported the data. However, no specific reason was found to suspect that such tactics were employed. On the contrary, the data show that the teams did not engage in any uniform rigging practice; otherwise, Group III in Table 14 would not have come out with an inferior crime control rating.

## ARREST PRODUCTIVITY

An early report under this study showed that neighborhood police team patrolmen had a higher number of arrests per man for felonies and mis-demeanors than their host precinct patrolmen in a four-month period in 1971.[6]

---

6.    Ibid.

Table 16 indicates that arrests per man were again significantly higher for all groups of team patrolmen for the three-month period April through June 1972 for robbery, felonies, and all arrests (felonies, misdemeanors, traffic violations, and summonses). The groups of teams are arranged chronologically by date of implementation (see note 1, Table 16) to test whether the arrest rate might be higher for teams that were in operation longer. Since such a tendency was not found in the data, arrest rates are probably more dependent on other factors such as the crime rate, team leadership, etc. Both the 6th Precinct team and the oldest team of the 77th Precinct have higher robbery arrest rates but lower felony and total arrests rates than their precincts as a whole. This may in part be due to the fact that both these teams have experienced large decreases in reported crime.

One hypothesis to explain the higher arrest rate by team patrolmen is that they are younger and thus more enthusiastic than other host precinct patrolmen. To examine the possibility of such a seniority bias, a comparison was made of arrests and summonses in Precinct 34 by 142 street patrolmen both before and after Operation Neighborhood was implemented in the entire precinct. The data (Table 17) indicate a significant increase under team policing in all categories of arrests and summonses.[7] Total arrests were up 44.3 percent; total summonses up 108.7 percent.

The substantial increase in parking summonses requires special consideration. First, such an increase may cause public antagonism toward the police. Second, this particular increase may reflect the controversy over summons quotas in the 5th Division which led division policemen (including those in Precinct 34) to greatly expand their parking summons activity.

7. The results may be slightly biased by the fact that nineteen patrolmen were transferred out of the precinct during this period, some of them because of their low arrest productivity.

TABLE 16: ARRESTS PER MAN, FOR NEIGHBORHOOD POLICE TEAMS, HOST PRECINCTS, AND COMPARISON PRECINCTS, APRIL THOUGH JUNE 1972[1]

| CRIME CATEGORY | TEAMS AND HOST PRECINCTS[2] | | | | | | | | | | | | ALL TEAM PRECINCTS | | COMPARISON PRECINCTS | |
|---|---|---|---|---|---|---|---|---|---|---|---|---|---|---|---|---|
| | Group I[3] | | Group II | | Group III | | Group IV | | 6th Precinct | | 77th Precinct[4] | | 34th | 24th | 114th | 79th |
| | Team | Precinct | Team | Precinct | Team | Precinct | Team | Precinct | Team | Precinct | Team | Precinct | | | | |
| Robbery | .17 | .09 | .26 | .11 | .38 | .16 | .11 | .10 | .31 | .14 | .69 | .25 | .27 | .27 | .10 | .30 |
| All Felonies | 1.09 | .68 | 1.05 | .21 | 1.42 | .88 | .95 | .73 | .28 | .90 | 1.10 | 1.19 | .76 | 1.42 | .44 | 1.92 |
| All Arrests | 2.62 | 1.59 | 2.84 | 1.62 | 4.01 | 1.56 | 2.04 | 1.52 | 1.67 | 1.29 | 1.76 | 2.30 | 1.56 | 2.80 | 1.15 | 3.54 |

1. "Arrests per man" was calculated using the number of arrests for the three-month period divided by the number of men in each group on patrol during the month of June. Includes only arrests made by plainclothes or uniformed street patrolmen; does not include arrests by anti-crime, detectives or other special units. The data for host precincts include crimes reported in team areas.

2. "Host precinct" refers to the precincts in which the teams are located.

3. See Table 14, page 38, for a definition of the groups.

4. "Team" in the 77th Precinct denotes crime data for the first team established in that precinct on January 1, 1971. "Precinct" denotes the reamining five teams established in the rest of the precinct on April 4, 1972. It should also be noted that the 77th was reorganized to include the 80th Precinct on this date and the data for the precinct are based on estimates of 1971 crime for the larger area.

TABLE 17: PERCENTAGE CHANGE IN ARRESTS AND SUMMONSES BY PRECINCT 34 PATROLMEN BEFORE AND AFTER IMPLEMENTATION OF OPERATION NEIGHBORHOOD[1]

| | Crime Category | January-May 1971 (Before) | January-May 1972 (After) | Number Increase | Percent Change |
|---|---|---|---|---|---|
| ARRESTS | Felonies | 151 | 204 | 53 | +35.1 |
| | Misdemeanor | 169 | 252 | 83 | +49.1 |
| | Others | 50 | 78 | 28 | +56.0 |
| | Total | 370 | 534 | 164 | +44.3 |
| SUMMONSES | Parking | 13,323 | 28,639 | 15,316 | +114.9 |
| | Moving | 1,516 | 2,401 | 885 | +58.4 |
| | Other | 115 | 257 | 102 | +65.8 |
| | Total | 14,994 | 31,397 | 16,303 | +108.7 |

1. Entire precinct came under team policing in August 1971. The comparisons are for January through May of 1971 and 1972. The 142 patrolmen in the study included only those who were on street patrol in the 34th Precinct in both 1971 and 1972.

Table 18 compares total arrests for the first five months of 1971 and 1972 in the all-team Precinct 34 with two comparison precincts (79 and 114) and the citywide data. The reduction in number of arrests accompanies a manpower reduction of approximately 10 percent in the department from 1971 to 1972. Although Precinct 34 arrests were down in all categories overall, the men who were patrolmen in both 1971 and 1972 were making more arrests, as described earlier.

Arrest rates for the all-team precincts, 24 and 34, were both lower than for comparison Precinct 79, a high crime precinct; but they were both higher than for comparison Precinct 114, a low crime precinct (see Table 16). Consequently, no firm conclusions on the effect of the team program can be drawn from these data.

A much more accurate measure of the effect of the program on arrest productivity can be derived from the before-and-after study of Precinct 34 (discussed above and detailed in Table 17). Consideration should be given to collecting these data on a regular basis.

TABLE 18: ARREST PRODUCTIVITY COMPARISONS CITYWIDE, ALL-TEAM PRECINCT, AND TWO OTHER PRECINCTS, FIRST FIVE MONTHS OF 1971 AND 1972

| CRIME CATEGORY | CITYWIDE | | | ALL-TEAM OPERATION Precinct 34 | | | COMPARISON PRECINCTS Precinct 79 | | | Precinct 114 | | |
|---|---|---|---|---|---|---|---|---|---|---|---|---|
| | 1971 | 1972 | % Change | 1971 | 1972 | % Change | 1971 | 1972 | % Change | 1971 | 1972 | % Change |
| Felonies | 43,556 | 41,796 | – 4.1 | 413 | 376 | – 9.0 | 1,008 | 1,009 | 0.0 | 496 | 448 | – 9.7 |
| Misdemeanors | 41,501 | 34,668 | –16.5 | 426 | 393 | – 7.7 | 517 | 467 | – 9.7 | 411 | 412 | 0.0 |
| Others* | 20,868 | 14,668 | –31.4 | 183 | 147 | –19.6 | 257 | 243 | – 5.4 | 310 | 160 | –48.4 |
| Total | 105,925 | 95,743 | – 9.6 | 1,022 | 916 | –11.4 | 1,782 | 1,719 | – 3.5 | 1,217 | 1,020 | –16.2 |

*Includes arrests by other authorities such as the Housing Authority Police.

Source: FBI Statistics.

IV

SUPERVISION

Neighborhood police teams in general vary in size from 25 to 45 men and are responsible for from 15 to 20 percent of the area of a precinct. Their workload varies from 8 to 30 percent of the precinct workload.

The guidelines for Operation Neighborhood state: "The team commander, whether or not he is on duty, is responsible for the activities of the team patrolmen." This imposes an unaccustomed responsibility on sergeants who become team commanders.

The guidelines suggest that the team commander should use two techniques to assist him in this supervisory task. First, team patrolmen are made "responsible for reporting to the team commander all incidents in which they encountered difficulties." Second, the team commander is responsible for conferring with sergeants and other superior officers who have observed the team patrolmen in the performance of their duties.

According to observations by the evaluators, these two procedures are not used by all team commanders. A number of possible explanations for this may be given:

- Sergeants' inexperience with expanded supervisory role

- The lack of adequate training of sergeants and patrolmen in their responsibilities

- The failure of precinct and team commanders to develop cooperation with other sergeants and superior officers

- The shortage of manpower in many precincts (especially during summer vacation periods).

All of these problems may be reduced by the Operation Neighborhood training program, which commenced after the data for this study were collected.

## PRECINCT COORDINATION

One of the most important supervisory problems in the program is developing good relationships among the team commander, the operations officer (a lieutenant), and the shift sergeants. Chart 2 shows the organization of Precinct 34 under Operation Neighborhood. Because the adequacy of this arrangement seemed questionable, another arrangement (see Chart 3) designed to minimize personnel conflicts was discussed early in the evaluation. A further observation is that a precinct commander can provide the leadership to resolve conflicts, whatever the chain of command. But the department still should seek to adopt the optimum form of organization.

Chart 3 indicates that lieutenants would have the responsibility of receiving reports from team commanders (they should confer with the commanders regularly, perhaps for one hour every week or two). Simultaneously, the lieutenants would be responsible for supervising an assigned number of shift sergeants (requiring about three hours total time every two weeks). Joint supervision of shift sergeants and team commanders is considered more likely to facilitate cooperation among them.

Under this arrangement, the sergeants who are not team commanders would share responsibility for the teams. In the 24th Precinct, Deputy Inspector Norman Anderson already has such an arrangement. He has assigned each of his shift sergeants to help evaluate team members in the precinct. That is, every six months each team commander is to file personnel reports on all his patrolmen. In addition, each shift sergeant is to file a report

CHART 2: ORGANIZATIONAL CHART FOR THE 34TH PRECINCT

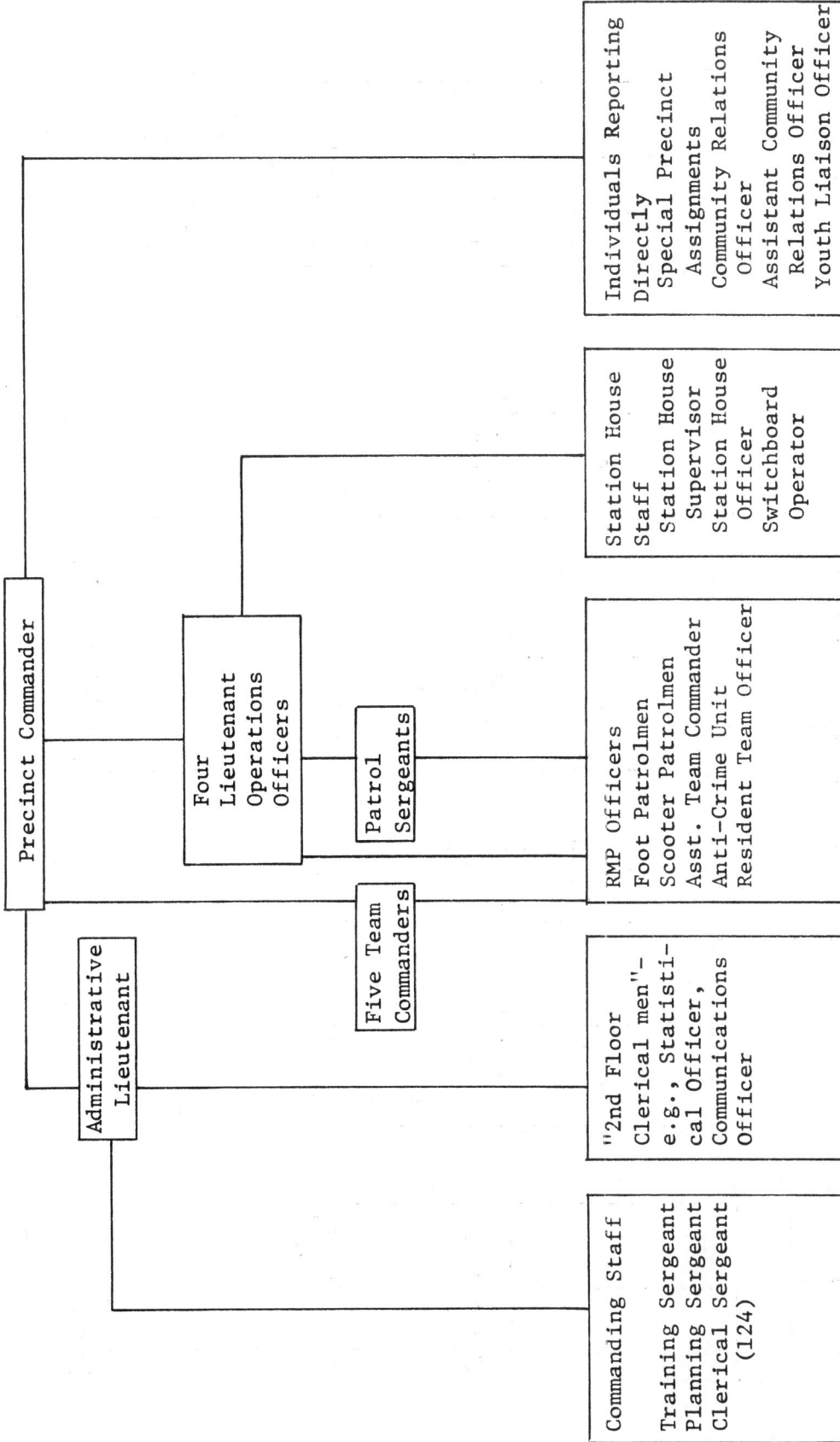

```
                                    ┌──────────────────┐
                                    │ Precinct Commander│
                                    └──────────────────┘
                                             │
        ┌────────────────────────┬───────────┼──────────────────┬──────────────────────┐
        │                        │           │                  │
┌───────────────┐      ┌──────────────────┐  │         ┌──────────────┐       ┌──────────────────┐
│Administrative │      │ Four             │  │         │ Station House│       │ Individuals      │
│Lieutenant     │      │ Lieutenant       │  │         │ Staff        │       │ Reporting        │
└───────────────┘      │ Operations       │  │         │              │       │ Directly         │
        │              │ Officers         │  │         │ Station House│       │                  │
        │              └──────────────────┘  │         │ Supervisor   │       │ Special Precinct │
        │                   │      │          │         │ Station House│       │ Assignments      │
        │              ┌─────────┐ │    ┌──────────┐    │ Officer      │       │ Community Relations│
        │              │ Patrol  │ │    │Five Team │    │ Switchboard  │       │ Officer          │
        │              │Sergeants│ │    │Commanders│    │ Operator     │       │ Assistant Community│
        │              └─────────┘ │    └──────────┘    └──────────────┘       │ Relations Officer │
        │                   │      │        │                                   │ Youth Liaison Officer│
┌───────────────┐  ┌────────────┐  │  ┌──────────────────┐                     └──────────────────┘
│Commanding Staff│ │"2nd Floor  │  │  │ RMP Officers     │
│               │ │Clerical men"│  │  │ Foot Patrolmen   │
│Training Sergeant│ │e.g., Statisti-│ │ Scooter Patrolmen│
│Planning Sergeant│ │cal Officer, │  │ Asst. Team Commander│
│Clerical Sergeant│ │Communications│ │ Anti-Crime Unit  │
│(124)           │ │Officer      │  │ Resident Team Officer│
└───────────────┘  └────────────┘     └──────────────────┘
```

Precinct Commander

Administrative Lieutenant

Four Lieutenant Operations Officers

Patrol Sergeants

Five Team Commanders

Station House Staff
Station House Supervisor
Station House Officer
Switchboard Operator

Individuals Reporting Directly
Special Precinct Assignments
Community Relations Officer
Assistant Community Relations Officer
Youth Liaison Officer

Commanding Staff
Training Sergeant
Planning Sergeant
Clerical Sergeant (124)

"2nd Floor Clerical men"—e.g., Statistical Officer, Communications Officer

RMP Officers
Foot Patrolmen
Scooter Patrolmen
Asst. Team Commander
Anti-Crime Unit
Resident Team Officer

CHART 3: OPERATION NEIGHBORHOOD PRECINCT (LIEUTENANTS IN STAFF POSITIONS)

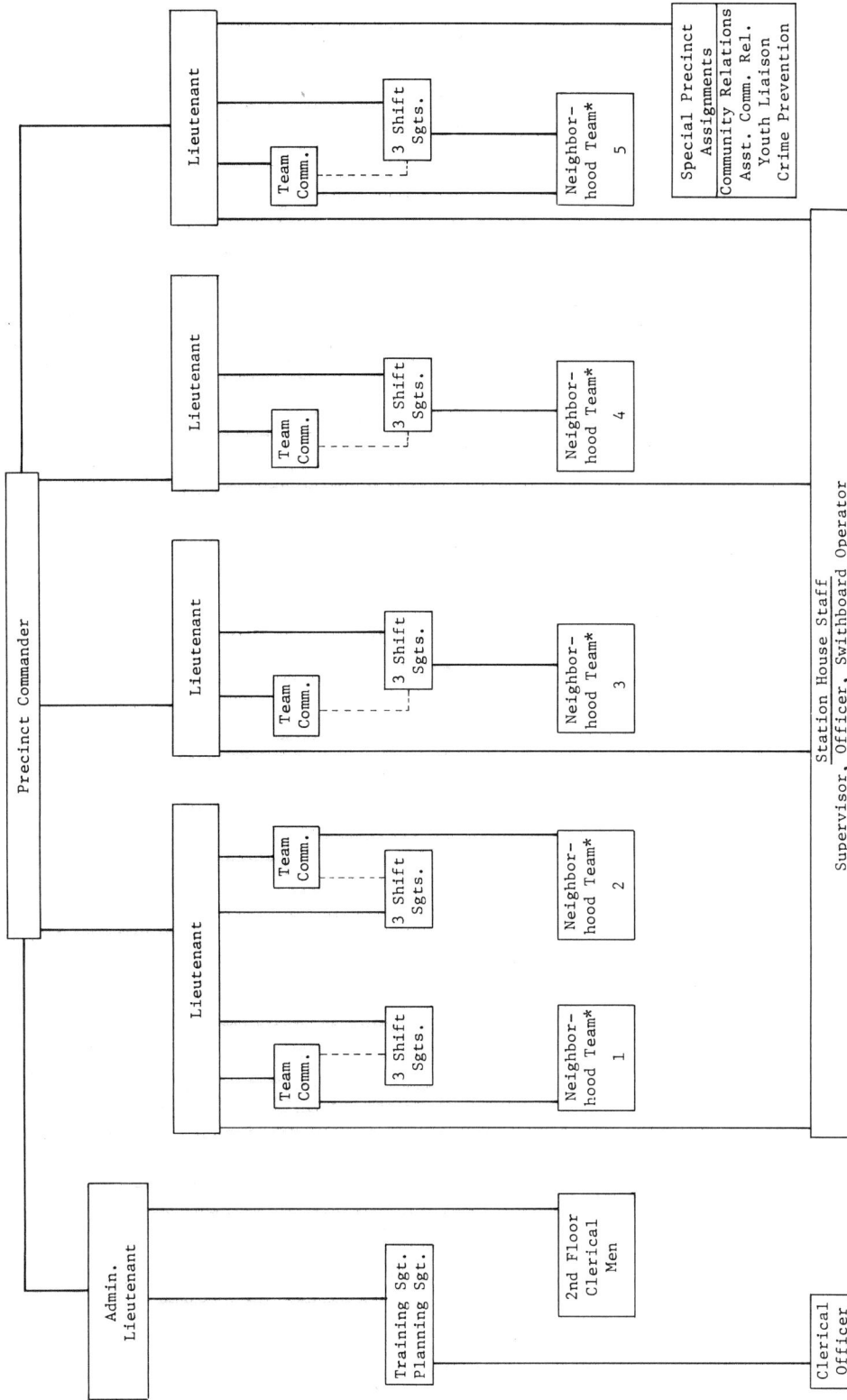

Precinct Commander

Admin. Lieutenant

Training Sgt.
Planning Sgt.

2nd Floor
Clerical Men

Clerical Officer

Lieutenant

Team Comm.

3 Shift Sgts.

Neighborhood Team* 1

Lieutenant

Team Comm.

3 Shift Sgts.

Neighborhood Team* 2

Lieutenant

Team Comm.

3 Shift Sgts.

Neighborhood Team* 3

Lieutenant

Team Comm.

3 Shift Sgts.

Neighborhood Team* 4

Lieutenant

Team Comm.

3 Shift Sgts.

Neighborhood Team* 5

Special Precinct
Assignments
Community Relations
Asst. Comm. Rel.
Youth Liaison
Crime Prevention

Station House Staff
Supervisor, Officer, Swithboard Operator

*All neighborhood teams include anti-crime (plainclothes) men.

on one-third of the patrolmen on each team. Placing a lieutenant in charge
of both the team commander and the shift sergeants would facilitate the combining of these reports into a more meaningful evaluation.

Under the proposed organization of the precinct, the precinct commander's
span of control is accomplished through only five persons. Under the plan
now being used in the 34th Precinct, it is difficult to count the number of
people reporting directly to the precinct commander, but the number exceeds 15.

A slight modification of Chart 3 presents a third option for organizing
a precinct to manage Operation Neighborhood: make each of the lieutenants a
team commander with a sergeant assisting in the administration and supervision of each of the four teams. This might require the assignment of one
additional lieutenant in a precinct currently having only five lieutenants.
If there were six teams, two additional lieutenants might be required. The
lieutenant would have direct responsibility as a team commander while retain-
ing his operational responsibilities as a lieutenant operations officer. In
the previous method, following Chart 3 as it is shown, the lieutenant would
have staff responsibility for team commanders, but he would not himself
command the team.

If lieutenants were made team commanders, their combined responsibilities might be considered too great. The precinct commander might find
personnel better suited for team leaders if he can select five or six from
an available pool of 21 sergeants rather than having to rely automatically
on all of the precinct lieutenants as team commanders.

The patrol services bureau is presently planning to experiment with
lieutenants as team commanders. Six lieutenants will serve as team commanders, and one will remain exclusively as operations lieutenant. Three
sergeants will be assigned to each lieutenant as assistant team commanders

and each will have responsibility for evaluating a squad of men (one-third of the team). This system is intended to shorten the span of control and also to integrate the lieutenants and shift sergeants into the Operation Neighborhood program.

The 34th Precinct has changed its organization slightly and now has a lieutenant coordinating all of the teams. The position of coordinator was initiated in the 24th Precinct; it appeared sufficiently valuable to be used in the 34th Precinct as well.

## USE OF TEAM CONFERENCES

Guidelines for Operation Neighborhood require team commanders to "hold frequent group conferences with members of the team. At these conferences, problems, conditions or any other matters affecting the operation of the sector shall be discussed." Later in the guidelines it is made clear that the team patrolman has a "responsibility to make suggestions or criticisms for improving the operation of the team."

The intention of these guidelines is to generate a new relationship between team commanders and their patrolmen. The patrolman is to hold a position of respect from which he can interact with his supervisor. He should not feel, as one patrolman reported on the patrol management survey, that he is being treated like a boy scout despite his life-and-death responsibilities as a patrolman.

In recent reports, 13 neighborhood teams reported that they were holding regular meetings with their patrolmen. (Sixteen teams appeared not to be holding such meetings, according to their reports.) When meetings were held, it is not clear how much interaction actually took place. For example, the evaluators have indirect information that in at least one part of the program, the meetings are one-way communications only. That is, team commanders give orders to their patrolmen without any interchange of information.

The 24th Precinct has arranged a format for meetings that may be giving an opportunity for interaction. These meetings last for two hours and and include some in-service training. They are held once each month and are attended by two-thirds of each team. That is, each month one-third of the team is not able to attend the conference.

## QUALITY OF SUPERVISION

A patrol management survey was carried out to measure the quality of supervision in Operation Neighborhood. (See Tables 19 and 20.) The results are mixed.

Prior to receiving the results of the survey, an Index of Quality of Supervision was constructed to help indicate whether supervision had been improved within the program. This index combines a number of questions relevant to the quality of supervision. (For a more detailed description of how the indexes were constructed, see Appendix C.)

On Tables 19 and 20, both Precinct 24 and Precinct 6 scored higher (indicating better supervision) than all comparison groups combined. Seniority was also statistically important, with more senior men scoring lower (quality of supervision poorer) than the younger men.

TABLE 19: INDEX OF QUALITY OF SUPERVISION*
(Adjusted for Seniority)

| OPERATION NEIGHBORHOOD | | COMPARISON GROUPS | |
|---|---|---|---|
| | Overall Mean | | Overall Mean |
| Volunteers | 104.6 | All Comparison Groups Combined | 102.8 |
| Precinct 6 | 106.7 | | |
| Precinct 34 | 104.6 | | |
| Precinct 24 | 108.2 | | |

*Higher scores indicate more professional, interactive supervision.

TABLE 20:   INDEX OF QUALITY OF SUPERVISION

(Raw June Scores, before Seniority Adjustments)

| OPERATION NEIGHBORHOOD | | COMPARISON GROUPS | |
|---|---|---|---|
| | June | | June |
| Volunteers | 104.6 | Comparison | 99.9 |
| Precinct 6 | 106.7 | Precinct 114 | 104.2 |
| Precinct 34 | 103.4 | Precinct 79 | 102.5 |
| Precinct 24 | 107.8 | | |

Standard Deviation = 8.00

The question which caused most of the difference on this index was Question 33:  "Is there one sergeant assigned to your precinct to whom you regularly talk about your job and your job problems?"[8]  On this question, the volunteers, Precinct 24 and Precinct 6 all had more "yes" answers than the comparisons.  While Precinct 34 had a larger proportion of "yes" answers than the comparisons, it had a smaller proportion than the comparison Precincts 79 or 114.  (The difference with Precinct 114 was significant; see Table 21.)  Therefore, Operation Neighborhood increased the likelihood of contacts with sergeants, but frequent contacts also can be found outside of the program.

TABLE 21:   NUMBER OF OFFICERS REPORTING REGULAR JOB
DISCUSSIONS WITH ONE SERGEANT

| OPERATION NEIGHBORHOOD | | | COMPARISON GROUPS | | |
|---|---|---|---|---|---|
| | Yes | No | | Yes | No |
| Volunteers | 28 | 8 | Comparisons | 5 | 10 |
| Precinct 6 | 33 | 5 | Precinct 114 | 9 | 4 |
| Precinct 34 | 8 | 9 | Precinct 79 | 7 | 6 |
| Precinct 24 | 14 | 5 | | | |
| Total | 83 | 27 | Total | 21 | 20 |
| Percent | 75.5 | 24.5 | Percent | 51.2 | 48.8 |

8.   See Patrol Management Survey, Appendix B.

Considering the extent to which neighborhood teams report that they have more regular contact with a sergeant, there are very few other indicators that the expected changes in patterns of supervision have occurred. It was a goal of Operation Neighborhood that the pattern of leadership would become more democratic or professional and less authoritarian. Therefore, the researchers expected a greater disbelief in the principle that "a good leader should be strict with people under him in order to improve their performance." The comparison groups tended to be neutral in their reactions to this principle. On the other hand, most of the other groups leaned toward mildly disagreeing. Precincts 6, 24 and the comparison Precinct 114 all disagreed more often with this principle than did the comparisons (i.e., non-volunteers).

TABLE 22:  PATROLMEN'S OPINIONS ON "STRICT LEADERSHIP"

(Adjusted for Seniority of 3 years or less)

What is your reaction to the principle that, "A good leader should be strict with people under him in order to improve their performance."?  (1) strongly agree (2) mildly agree (3) not sure  (4) mildly disagree and (5) strongly disagree.

| OPERATION NEIGHBORHOOD | | | | | COMPARISON GROUPS | |
|---|---|---|---|---|---|---|
| | Overall Mean | January | April | June | | Overall Mean |
| Volunteers | 3.56 | | | | Comparisons | 3.19 |
| Precinct 6 | 4.09 | | | | Precinct 114 | 3.68 |
| Precinct 34 | 3.59 | 3.86 | 3.15 | 3.66 | Precinct 79 | 3.61 |

NOTE: On this table, and all other tables presenting results from a single question, point values were assigned to responses so that the number of the response equals the number of points; e.g., response 3 was assigned a value of 3 points.

It was also hoped that the availability of a team commander would lead to the systematic development of management information about how well the patrolmen were doing. When patrolmen were asked how much their superiors knew about their job performance, only the patrolmen in Precinct 6 gave their supervisors a higher knowledgeability rating than did the patrolmen who served as comparisons or who worked in Precinct 114. In addition, Precinct 34 showed deterioration on this question in the June interview. The reasons for this deterioration probably were the small number of sergeants available in the precinct and the need to have team commanders double as shift sergeants.

TABLE 23: KNOWLEDGE BY SUPERIORS ABOUT PATROLMEN'S JOB PERFORMANCE
(Adjusted for the Log of Seniority)

"How much do your superiors know about how well you do your job?"

| (1) No one person knows enough to judge my work fairly | (2) They have some knowledge about how I do my job | (3) They know generally how well I do my job | (4) They are well informed about most things I do on the job | (5) They are well informed about everything I do on the job |

| OPERATION NEIGHBORHOOD | | | | COMPARISON GROUPS | | | | |
|---|---|---|---|---|---|---|---|---|
| | Overall Mean | January | April | June | | Overall Mean | January | April | June |
| Volunteers | 2.81 | 2.86 | 2.98 | 2.53 | Comparisons | 3.11 | 3.06 | 2.88 | 3.33 |
| Precinct 6 | 3.22 | | | 3.22 | | | | | |
| Precinct 34 | 2.80 | 3.02 | 2.84 | 2.39 | Precinct 114 | 2.82 | 2.80 | 2.62 | 3.07 |
| Precinct 24 | 2.90 | | | 2.90 | Precinct 79 | 2.43 | | 2.23 | 2.68 |

It had been hoped that members of the neighborhood police teams would find their supervisors more understanding and sympathetic and more receptive to suggestions. The receptivity to suggestions should have stimulated more suggestions by the patrolmen and should have resulted in more of those suggestions being acted upon by the team commanders. In fact, the survey showed none of these events occurring. Indeed, there was a slight tendency in Precinct 34 for team members to report their supervisors as being less understanding in each successive survey. This result could be attributed to the increasing demands placed on the team commanders in that period, causing them to be less available to their men.

Team commanders themselves made this point in meetings with Captain Mendyk of the Patrol Services Bureau. They indicated that the morale of their men decreased as they were pulled more often from normal work assignments. This disruption of team activity occurred, according to team commanders, because of manpower reduction in the different teams. This in turn reflected a general reduction of patrolmen. While understandable in this context, the "stealing" of men from neighborhood teams for other assignments certainly disrupted both supervisory activity and team morale.

V

## SATISFACTION WITH PAY AND WORK SCHEDULES

An important goal of Operation Neighborhood is to improve patrolmen's satisfaction with their job activities. If satisfaction with job activities makes patrolmen more satisfied with their pay and the hours they work, these attitudinal changes are important side effects of a program.

The guidelines for Operation Neighborhood gave team commanders the responsibility for formulating work hours and assigning patrolmen. Their first task was to allocate their manpower consistent with the workload. As the planning division of the New York City Police Department found in its August 1971 evaluation of the NPT Program, the commanders were successful in this matching of manpower to workload.

After ascertaining their manpower requirements, it then became the task of the team commanders to determine which hours individual patrolmen wished to work. While they could not force any patrolman to work hours that differed from the official charts established with the union, the commanders encouraged team members to deviate voluntarily from those charts. It is feasible, given good leadership, to develop manpower scheduling which is more satisfactory for many of the patrolmen included in a team.

Primarily as the result of increased satisfaction with their work schedules, patrolmen in Precinct 6 and in volunteer groups showed greater job satisfaction than all comparison groups on the Index of Extrinsic Job Satisfaction. (See Tables 24 and 25.)

TABLE 24:   INDEX OF EXTRINSIC JOB SATISFACTION

(Adjusted for Seniority of the Patrolmen)

| OPERATION NEIGHBORHOOD | | COMPARISON GROUPS | |
|---|---|---|---|
| | Overall Mean | | Overall Mean |
| Volunteers | 112.7 | All Comparison Groups Combined | 100.97 |
| Precinct 6 | 114.6 | | |
| Precinct 34 | 104.8 | | |
| Precinct 24 | 92.1 | | |

NOTE:   Higher numbers equal greater satisfaction.

TABLE 25:   INDEX OF EXTRINSIC JOB SATISFACTION

(Raw June Scores)

| OPERATION NEIGHBORHOOD | | COMPARISON GROUPS | |
|---|---|---|---|
| | June | | June |
| Volunteers | 113.0 | Comparisons | 88.5 |
| Precinct | 114.4 | Precinct 114 | 94.2 |
| Precinct 34 | 109.1 | Precinct 79 | 91.2 |
| Precinct 24 | 95.0 | | |

NOTE:   Higher numbers equal greater satisfaction.

Relatively speaking, the volunteers and Precinct 34 show greater satisfaction with their work schedule than do the comparison groups.   (See Table 26.)

TABLE 26: SATISFACTION WITH WORK SCHEDULES

(Adjusted for Seniority of the Patrolmen)

How satisfied are you with your work schedule?

1. Very  2. Somewhat  3. Mildly  4. Somewhat dissatisfied  5. Very dissatisfied

| | OPERATION NEIGHBORHOOD | | | | COMPARISON GROUPS | | | |
|---|---|---|---|---|---|---|---|---|
| | Overall Mean | January | April | June | Overall Mean | January | April | June |
| Volunteers | 2.88 | 3.19 | 3.00 | 2.46 | | | | |
| Precinct 6 | 3.05 | | | 3.05 | All Comparisons | | | |
| Precinct 34 | 2.66 | 2.84 | 2.38 | 2.70 | 3.41 | 3.31 | 2.85 | 3.17 |
| Precinct 24 | 3.41 | | | 3.41 | | | | |

Regarding pay satisfaction, Precinct 34 registers a relatively poor score. Precinct 6's relatively good score on pay satisfaction adds to its good showing on the index which combines both the pay and work schedule satisfaction (Tables 24 and 25).

TABLE 27: PAY SATISFACTION

(Adjusted for the Log of the Patrolmen's Seniority)

How satisfied are you with your pay?

| 1. Completely satisfied | 2. Generally satisfied | 3. Not too satisfied | 4. Dissatisfied | 5. Very dis-satisfied |
|---|---|---|---|---|

| OPERATION NEIGHBORHOOD | | COMPARISON GROUPS | |
|---|---|---|---|
| | Overall Mean | | Overall Mean |
| Volunteers | 3.29 | Precinct 114 | 3.71 |
| Precinct 6 | 3.26 | Comparisons and Precinct 79 | 3.32 |
| Precinct 34 | 3.68 | | |
| Precinct 24 | 3.93 | | |

TABLE 28:  SATISFACTION WITH CHANGE IN WORK SCHEDULE

In the last month, how satisfied were you with your work schedule compared to a year ago?

| 1. | Much less satisfied | 2. | A little less satisfied | 3. | About the same | 4. | A little more satisfied | 5. | Much more satisfied |

| OPERATION NEIGHBORHOOD | | COMPARISON GROUPS | |
|---|---|---|---|
| | Overall Mean | | Overall Mean |
| Volunteers | 3.43 | All Comparisons Groups Combined | 3.03 |
| Precinct 6 | 3.61 | | |
| Precinct 34 | 3.12 | | |
| Precinct 24 | 2.76 | | |

VI

CITIZEN COOPERATION

An important objective of Operation Neighborhood is to increase the cooperation which patrolmen receive from the public, particularly cooperation which will assist in the reduction of crime. For the purpose of the patrol management survey, several indexes were constructed to measure citizen cooperation. The Index of Citizen Cooperation (Table 29) includes only those questions which relate to citizen actions that would support the police.

It was not surprising, considering the length of time over which citizen attitudes have been formed, that the Index of Citizen Cooperation showed little improvement for the Operation Neighborhood groups. Precinct 34 showed a statistically important improvement, but the magnitude of the difference over all comparisons was only 1.8 points on the index. The most discouraging finding with this index was a significant deterioration in citizen cooperation between April and June in areas served by the volunteer teams.

TABLE 29:  INDEX OF CITIZEN COOPERATION
(Adjusted for Seniority of Patrolmen)

| OPERATION NEIGHBORHOOD | | | | | COMPARISON GROUPS | |
|---|---|---|---|---|---|---|
| | Overall Mean | January | April | June | Overall Mean | |
| Volunteers | 97.2 | 97.8 | 98.5 | 94.9 | | All Comparison Groups Combined |
| Precinct 6 | 97.6 | | | | 96.6 | |
| Precinct 34 | 98.4 | | | | | |
| Precinct 24 | 99.0 | | | | | |

NOTE:  Higher numbers equal greater cooperation.

Notice that the Index of Citizen Cooperation (Raw Scores, Table 30) shows Precinct 114 with a very low score.

TABLE 30:   INDEX OF CITIZEN CRIME COOPERATION

(Raw Scores)

| OPERATION NEIGHBORHOOD | | COMPARISON GROUPS | |
|---|---|---|---|
| | June | | June |
| Volunteers | 95.5 | Comparisons | 94.3 |
| Precinct 6 | 96.3 | Precinct 114 | 92.9 |
| Precinct 34 | 96.6 | Precinct 79 | 95.5 |
| Precinct 24 | 98.2 | | |

NOTE:  Higher numbers equal greater cooperation.  Standard Deviation = 6.7

The Operation Neighborhood groups all reported a higher level of cooperation from the public than did comparison groups.  (See Table 31.)

TABLE 31:   CITIZEN COOPERATION IN PROVIDING CRIME INFORMATION

(Adjusted for the Log of the Seniority of Patrolmen)

How cooperative has the public been lately when you needed information about a crime?

1.  Almost    2.  Seldom   3.  Sometimes    4.  Usually   5.  Almost
    never          help         help             help          always
    help                                                       help

| OPERATION NEIGHBORHOOD | | COMPARISON GROUPS | |
|---|---|---|---|
| | Overall Mean | | Overall Mean |
| Volunteers | 2.95 | All Comparison Groups Combined | 2.63 |
| Precinct 6 | 2.97 | | |
| Precinct 34 | 3.03 | | |
| Precinct 24 | 3.10 | | |

Informants used by the police generally include two classes of people: those who are paid for providing information and those who may avoid prosecution for their own offenses by cooperating with the police.

It appears from Table 32 that somewhat greater use was being made of informants by the Operation Neighborhood groups, compared to the comparisons and Precinct 114 combined.  However, Precinct 79 (a comparison precinct) also used substantially more informants than the rest of the comparison groups.

### TABLE 32:   NUMBER OF INFORMANTS SUPPLYING CRIME INFORMATION
#### (Adjusted for Seniority of Patrolmen)

How many <u>informants</u> have given you information about criminals or criminal activities <u>in the last month</u>?

| OPERATION NEIGHBORHOOD | | COMPARISON GROUPS | |
|---|---|---|---|
| | Overall Mean | | Overall Mean |
| Volunteers | 12.1 | Precinct 79 | 16.8 |
| Precinct 6 | 14.0 | Comparisons | |
| Precinct 34 | 15.1 | and Precinct 114 | 9.2 |
| Precinct 24 | 17.5 | | |

In addition to informants, Operation Neighborhood seeks to reach out to ordinary people who are not paid or given special consideration.  Precincts 34 and 24 enjoy some advantage over Precincts 114 and 79 combined, but the success of this effort to reach the people is not clear.  (See Table 33.)

### TABLE 33:   ORDINARY PEOPLE (NOT INFORMANTS) SUPPLYING CRIME INFORMATION
#### (Adjusted for Seniority of Patrolmen)

How many people <u>other than informants</u> whom you talk to on a regular basis have given you information about criminals or criminal activities <u>in the last month</u>?

| OPERATION NEIGHBORHOOD | | COMPARISON GROUPS | |
|---|---|---|---|
| | Overall Mean | | Overall Mean |
| Volunteers | 2.42 | Comparisons | 2.55 |
| Precinct 6 | 1.92 | Precinct 114 | |
| Precinct 34 | 2.59 | and Precinct 79 | 2.04 |
| Precinct 24 | 3.19 | | |

It is widely known that not all crimes committed are reported to the police.  For this reason, the patrolmen were asked how likely they thought it was that people would report a petty theft to the police.  No differences were found among the groups; both the volunteers and the patrolmen in Precinct 114 indicated, in successive interviews, that citizen cooperation in this area was rapidly declining.

TABLE 34: PERCENT OF CITIZENS BELIEVED WILLING TO REPORT A PETTY THEFT
(Adjusted for Seniority of Patrolmen)

In your opinion, about what percent of people who had a $40 item stolen from their car would report the incident to the police?

| OPERATION NEIGHBORHOOD | | | | | COMPARISON GROUPS | | | | |
|---|---|---|---|---|---|---|---|---|---|
| | Mean Percent | | | | | Mean Percent | | | |
| | Overall | Jan. | April | June | | Overall | Jan. | April | June |
| Volunteers | 58.9 | 75.7 | 56.3 | 46.4 | Precinct 114 | 64.4 | 80.1 | 64.9 | 53.2 |
| Precinct 6 | 55.9 | | | | Comparisons and | | | | |
| Precinct 34 | 52.4 | | | | Precinct 79 | 49.6 | | | |
| Precinct 24 | 44.4 | | | | | | | | |

VII

THE ATTITUDE OF POLICE OFFICERS TOWARD THE COMMUNITY


An index was constructed to measure whether patrolmen in Operation
Neighborhood would be, as hoped, more oriented toward service to the public,
more inclined toward tactics which involved getting information from people,[9]
and less inclined toward aggressive tactics such as stop-and-frisk or
questioning suspicious individuals.

There is, of course, a considerable body of opinion among both the
police and the community that police can give better protection by engaging
in some of these aggressive tactics. An ultimate hope of team policing,
however, is that increasing emphasis will be placed on activities which are
both productive and related to community relations. Data from the surveys
do not indicate that Operation Neighborhood patrolmen have advanced any
further in this direction than other police. (See Tables 35 and 36.)

TABLE 35: INDEX OF COMMUNITY-ORIENTED ATTITUDES
(Adjusted for Seniority* of the Patrolmen)

| OPERATION NEIGHBORHOOD | | | | COMPARISON GROUPS | | | |
|---|---|---|---|---|---|---|---|
| | January | April | June | | January | April | June |
| Volunteers | 133.8 | 132.6 | 135.3 | Comparisons | 137.1 | 133.9 | 131.2 |
| Precinct 6 | | | 131.1 | Precinct 114 | 134.7 | 133.0 | 133.2 |
| Precinct 34 | 135.5 | 130.7 | 133.7 | Precinct 79 | | 134.4 | 131.7 |
| Precinct 24 | | | 131.9 | | | | |

*Seniority is particularly strong for this variable. If a group had a
patrolman with eight years of seniority, its score in the June wave would
be calculated by deducting .6 from this table.

---

9. Because of the increased importance to be attached to service and
to gathering information from citizens, it was thought that comparatively
less importance would be attached to traditional techniques such as "observing
things carefully."

TABLE 36:   INDEX OF COMMUNITY-ORIENTED ATTITUDES

(Raw Scores)

| OPERATION NEIGHBORHOOD | | COMPARISON GROUPS | |
|---|---|---|---|
| | June | | June |
| Volunteers | 134.4 | Comparisons | 129.2 |
| Precinct 6 | 132.0 | Precinct 114 | 130.7 |
| Precinct 34 | 134.3 | Precinct 79 | 134.7 |
| Precinct 24 | 133.7 | | |

For the department as a whole, in fact, there was a consistent deterioration over time on this index, indicating perhaps that patrolmen were becoming less oriented toward community service (as defined in this research).

The team commanders were supposed to place somewhat more emphasis on foot patrol as a way of placing the patrolmen in close contact with the community and developing leads for gaining information about crime.  Of course, this was during a period of declining manpower within the New York City Police Department, and it was difficult for the commanders to find the men to place on foot patrol.  One precinct, located in Greenwich Village, was an exception.  In Precinct 6, more foot patrol was used and the men placed greater value on foot patrol than did other patrolmen in the Operation Neighborhood program and in the comparison groups.  (See Table 37.)

TABLE 37:   RELATIVE IMPORTANCE OF FOOT PATROL* TO PATROLMEN

(Scores are Adjusted for Seniority of the Patrolmen)

| OPERATION NEIGHBORHOOD | | COMPARISON GROUPS | |
|---|---|---|---|
| | Overall Mean | | Overall Mean |
| Volunteers | 2.63 | All Comparison Groups Combined | 2.84 |
| Precinct 6 | 1.89 | | |
| Precinct 34 | 2.53 | | |
| Precinct 24 | 2.43 | | |

*This item was ranked with six other items.  A low numerical score indicates a high value placed on foot patrol.

Aggressive patrol practices may be viewed in two ways.  On the one hand, they are an indication that the patrolman is conscientious in performing his duty and is not loafing on the job.  On the other hand, they are an indication that a police team is willing to engage in tactics which may, in the long run, result in incidents which will antagonize the community.  Generally, aggressive patrol practices result in incidents that occur on the street and that are observed by bystanders.  Therefore, it is of some concern that patrolmen in Precincts 6, 34 and 24 all report a significantly greater use of aggressive patrol practices than do the patrolmen in the comparison groups.  (See Table 38.)  The volunteers reported a high degree of aggressive patrol when they were interviewed in January.  As Table 38 shows, however, their use of aggressive patrol declined considerably from January through June and the volunteers became an exception to the tendency of Operation Neighborhood teams to report greater use of aggressive patrol practices.

TABLE 38:  FREQUENCY OF PATROLMAN'S OWN USE OF AGGRESSIVE PATROL PRACTICES

In the last month, how often have you practiced aggressive patrol practices such as stop-and-frisk.

1.  Almost never   2.  Seldom   3.  Sometimes   4.  Often   5.  Very often

| OPERATION NEIGHBORHOOD | | | | | COMPARISON GROUPS | | | | |
|---|---|---|---|---|---|---|---|---|---|
| | Overall Mean | Jan. | April | June | | Overall Mean | Jan. | April | June |
| Volunteers | 2.25 | 2.76 | 2.22 | 1.82 | All Comparison Groups Combined | 2.40 | 2.65 | 2.14 | 2.21 |
| Precinct 6 | 2.90 | | | | | | | | |
| Precinct 34 | 2.90 | | | | | | | | |
| Precinct 24 | 2.98 | | | | | | | | |

On a related question, officers were asked to tell how effective they thought the precinct had been recently in using aggressive patrol practices.  A report that the precinct did not use such practices was given the score zero.  In general, Operation Neighborhood groups tended to rate the effectiveness of aggressive patrol higher than comparison groups. As indicated in Table 39, the rating given by Precinct 6 patrolmen was particularly high.

TABLE 39:  PATROLMAN'S ESTIMATE OF THE EFFECTIVENESS OF AGGRESSIVE PATROL
(Adjusted for Seniority of the Patrolmen)

In the last month, how effective have precinct police been in preventing crime by aggressive patrol practices such as stop-and-frisk?

| 0. Not applicable (the precinct does not use these techniques) | 1. Very ineffective | 2. Somewhat effective | 3. Reasonably effective | 4. Very effective | 5. Extremely effective |
|---|---|---|---|---|---|

| OPERATION NEIGHBORHOOD | | COMPARISON GROUPS | |
|---|---|---|---|
| | Overall Mean | | Overall Mean |
| Volunteers | 3.57 | All Comparison Groups Combined | 3.20 |
| Precinct 6 | 4.08 | | |
| Precinct 34 | 3.56 | | |
| Precinct 24 | 2.91 | | |

Also of interest was whether patrolmen considered preventive patrol[10] effective. It was believed that, if team commanders encouraged effective use of other techniques (such as following up specific leads, stake-outs, plain-clothes patrol, or developing special sources of information in the community), then the policemen would place a relatively lower value on preventive patrol. That is, it was an hypothesis of Operation Neighborhood that, as more non-aggressive tactics were used, preventive patrol (the traditional method) would be less esteemed.

As Table 40 indicates, only the volunteers appear to have moved in this direction. In June the volunteers attached less importance to preventive patrol than they did in April or January. (This development may reflect the introduction of more innovative techniques.) Since this finding relies

---

10. Preventive patrol is defined as riding or walking around a community and observing events carefully.

heavily on the seniority adjustment, it may be discounted somewhat. The un-adjusted data presented in Table 41 indicate that the members of Operation Neighborhood groups tend to believe that the precinct police have been effective in preventing crime by preventive patrol. There is, however, some ambiguity surrounding this question. Were respondents comparing their precinct to other precincts or were they actually rating the effectiveness of preventive patrol?

TABLE 40:   PATROLMAN'S ESTIMATE OF THE EFFECTIVENESS OF PREVENTIVE PATROL
(Adjusted for Seniority of the Patrolman)

In the last month, how effective have precinct police been in preventing crime by preventive patrol?

| 1. Very in-effective | 2. Somewhat effective | 3. Reasonably effective | 4. Very effective | 5. Extremely effective |
|---|---|---|---|---|

| OPERATION NEIGHBORHOOD | | | | COMPARISON GROUPS | | | |
|---|---|---|---|---|---|---|---|
| | January | April | June | | January | April | June |
| Volunteers | 2.79 | 2.81 | 2.23 | Precinct 114 | 4.43 | 5.91 | 2.64 |
| Precinct 6 | | | 2.73 | Comparisons and Precinct 79 | (Overall Mean) 3.15 | | |
| Precinct 34 | 2.37 | 1.54 | 3.23 | | | | |
| Precinct 24 | | | 3.88 | | | | |

TABLE 41:   PATROLMAN'S ESTIMATE OF THE EFFECTIVENESS OF PREVENTIVE PATROL
(Raw June Scores)

In the last month, how effective have precinct police been in preventing crime by preventive patrol?

| 1. Very in-effective | 2. Somewhat effective | 3. Reasonably effective | 4. Very effective | 5. Extremely effective |
|---|---|---|---|---|

| OPERATION NEIGHBORHOOD | | COMPARISON GROUPS | |
|---|---|---|---|
| | June | | June |
| Volunteers | 3.08 | Comparisons | 2.93 |
| Precinct 6 | 3.22 | Precinct 114 | 2.69 |
| Precinct 34 | 3.53 | Precinct 79 | 2.62 |
| Precinct 24 | 3.37 | | |

Conflicts between police and community members (especially young people) can develop over the issue of loitering. It was expected that team policemen would be more tolerant of groups of loiterers and, hence, would place less importance on breaking up such groups. The data in Table 42 indicate, however, that only one Operation Neighborhood group (Precinct 24) gave this activity a relatively high ranking. Evidently, Precinct 24 patrolmen believe that breaking up groups of loiterers is less important than other patrol activities. The difference between the ranking given by Precinct 24 patrolmen and the comparisons is statistically significant.

TABLE 42:  RELATIVE IMPORTANCE OF BREAKING UP GROUPS OF LOITERERS*

| OPERATION NEIGHBORHOOD | | | | | COMPARISON GROUPS | | | | |
|---|---|---|---|---|---|---|---|---|---|
| | Overall Mean | Jan. | April | June | | Overall Mean | Jan. | April | June |
| Volunteers | 4.88 | | | | Comparisons | 4.69 | 4.31 | 5.03 | 4.63 |
| Precinct 6 | 4.44 | | | | Precinct 114 | 5.08 | | | |
| Precinct 34 | 4.63 | 4.84 | 3.97 | 5.06 | Precinct 79 | 4.73 | | | |
| Precinct 24 | 5.39 | | | | | | | | |

*This item was ranked with six other items.  A low numerical score indicates a high ranking.  Scores are adjusted for seniority of the patrolmen.

While radio car patrol obviously takes up a large portion of a patrolman's time, some other activities are more innovative and perhaps more useful.  It was suspected that patrolmen in Operation Neighborhood would be more likely to place a relatively low value on radio car patrol, but the data do not indicate that this is true (see Table 43).

TABLE 43: RELATIVE IMPORTANCE OF RADIO CAR PATROL*

| OPERATION NEIGHBORHOOD | | COMPARISON GROUPS | |
|---|---|---|---|
| | Overall Mean | | Overall Mean |
| Volunteers | 1.42 | All Comparison Groups Combined | 1.72 |
| Precinct 6 | 1.74 | | |
| Precinct 34 | 1.61 | | |
| Precinct 24 | 1.35 | | |

*This item was ranked with six other items. A low numerical score indicates high ranking. Scores are adjusted for seniority of the patrolmen.

It was also hoped that the team commanders would be able to develop in their men a high regard for preliminary investigations. When Operation Neighborhood began, patrolmen did not as a rule perform investigations. However, the team commanders were given the flexibility to authorize their men to perform investigative activities.

In January 1972, the New York City Police Department issued a general order encouraging the patrol division to routinely begin preliminary investigations. Since neighborhood teams were already supposed to be engaging in this activity, they had a headstart and, theoretically a high regard for preliminary investigations. As Table 44 illustrates, Operation Neighborhood has had little success in increasing the importance of preliminary investigation in the eyes of patrolmen. (For volunteers, the ranking in June is lower than the one given in January.)

TABLE 44:  RELATIVE IMPORTANCE OF PRELIMINARY INVESTIGATION*

| OPERATION NEIGHBORHOOD | | | | | COMPARISON GROUPS | | | | |
|---|---|---|---|---|---|---|---|---|---|
| | Overall Mean | Jan. | April | June | | Overall Mean | Jan. | April | June |
| Volunteers | 4.55 | 4.33 | 4.40 | 4.95 | All Comparison Groups Combined | 4.48 | 4.95 | 4.44 | 4.07 |
| Precinct 6 | 4.26 | | | 4.26 | | | | | |
| Precinct 34 | 5.02 | 5.46 | 4.41 | 5.01 | | | | | |
| Precinct 24 | 4.27 | | | 4.27 | | | | | |

*This item was ranked with six other items.  A low numerical score indicates high ranking.  Scores are adjusted for seniority of the patrolmen.

NOTE:  Overall, the groups rated preliminary investigation as a little more important in each successive wave.  Department policy shifted this responsibility to the patrol division beginning in January.

Under Operation Neighborhood patrolmen are encouraged to park their vehicles in order to walk the streets and talk with the people.  Of course, in many precincts the workload is so high that patrolmen are reluctant to spend their time this way.  The data in Table 45 indicate that Precinct 6 and the volunteers rate this activity lower than do the remainder of the groups in the survey.  In Precinct 6, where there is somewhat greater use of foot patrol, this is somewhat understandable.  However, there is no explanation for why this effect has occurred among the volunteers.  It is encouraging to note that the "park, walk and talk" program is given greater importance by Precinct 34 than it is by all of the other groups in the survey.

TABLE 45:  RELATIVE IMPORTANCE OF "PARK, WALK AND TALK"

| | Overall Mean | Standard Error |
|---|---|---|
| Precinct 34 | 5.05 | 2.7 |
| All Other Groups | 5.75 | 2.0 |
| ************************************ | ******************** | |
| Precinct 6 | 6.26 | 4.8 |
| Volunteers | 5.84 | 2.8 |
| All Other Groups | 5.44 | 2.1 |

NOTE:  This item was ranked with six other items.  A low numerical score indicates high ranking.  Scores are adjusted for seniority of the patrolmen.

Because Operation Neighborhood was intended to increase the value placed by patrolmen on other activities, it was believed that team members would rank "observing everything carefully" lower than would other members of the department. As the data in Table 46 indicate, this did not happen.

TABLE 46: RELATIVE IMPORTANCE OF OBSERVING EVERYTHING CAREFULLY

| OPERATION NEIGHBORHOOD | | | | | COMPARISON GROUPS | |
|---|---|---|---|---|---|---|
| | Overall Mean | Jan. | April | June | | Overall Mean |
| Volunteers | 1.52 | | | | All Comparison Groups Combined | 1.97 |
| Precinct 6 | 1.32 | | | | | |
| Precinct 34 | 1.81 | 1.77 | 2.25 | 1.37 | | |
| Precinct 24 | 2.32 | | | | | |

NOTE: This item was ranked with six other items. A low numerical score indicates high ranking. Scores are adjusted for the log of a patrolman's seniority.

VIII

## GENERAL CITIZEN SUPPORT

Citizens can play an important role in the effort to reduce crime by actively cooperating with the police and providing useful information. Consequently, it is important for policemen to improve their relationships with individuals who are inclined to cooperate with them. But, as the data indicate, not all citizens are so inclined.[11] Some are basically hostile towards the police.

Cultivating citizen support may mean in some cases replacing indifference with cooperation. In other cases, it may mean merely lessening citizen hostility towards the police, so that they may accomplish their tasks with less opposition.

The chapter on citizen cooperation[12] was concerned with the impact of Operation Neighborhood on active citizen support, specifically the willingness of citizens to provide information directly related to crimes. This chapter, however, is concerned with the impact of Operation Neighborhood on general citizen support. Since both sides of the issue are vital, policemen as well as citizens were questioned. Citizen attitudes were measured by the community survey[13] and the police attitudes by the patrol survey.[14]

### RESULTS OF THE CITIZEN SURVEY

Citizen recognition of the Operation Neighborhood Program was quite high. In response to an open-ended question asking citizens whether they

11. See Tables 31, 33, 34, 61, 62, and 63.
12. This chapter begins on page 63.
13. See page 34 for detailed discussion on groups interviewed.
14. See Appendix B, page 135.

knew about any special programs which police were using, 39 percent of the businessmen interviewed in Precinct 34 spontaneously mentioned the Neighborhood Police Team Program. (See Table 47.) Citizens who did not spontaneously mention Operation Neighborhood or neighborhood police teams were asked if they had heard about neighborhood police teams. Once again, the businessmen in the 34th Precinct recorded a high level of recognition—29 percent. Recognition among residents and youth was substantial, but it was not as high as among businesmen. (This may be due to the greater ability of foot patrolmen to reach businessmen rather than residents.) Altogether, 68 percent of the businessmen in Precinct 34 had heard about Operation Neighborhood.

TABLE 47: PERCENT OF CITIZENS WHO HAD HEARD OF
OPERATION NEIGHBORHOOD OR TEAM POLICING

| RESPONSE | RESIDENTS | | BUSINESSMEN | | YOUTH | | COMMUNITY MEET-ING PARTICIPANTS 34th Precinct |
|---|---|---|---|---|---|---|---|
| | 34th Precinct | 114th Precinct | 34th Precinct | 114th Precinct | 34th Precinct | 114th Precinct | |
| Mentioned Operation Neighborhood or Team Policing | 13 | 0 | 39 | 0 | 10 | 0 | 56 |
| Recognized Team Policing After Prompting | 7 | 0 | 29 | 20 | 7 | 15 | 24 |
| Total Who Had Heard Of Operation Neighborhood | 20 | 0 | 68 | 20 | 17 | 15 | 80 |

Compared to their counterparts in Precinct 114, businessmen in the 34th precinct were more likely to know the name of a patrolman who worked in the neighborhood. (See Table 48.)

TABLE 48: PERCENT OF CITIZENS WHO DO AND DO NOT
KNOW THE NAME OF A PATROLMAN IN THEIR NEIGHBORHOOD
(Percent, followed by absolute numbers in parentheses)

Do you know the name of any policemen who work in this neighborhood?

| GROUP | Know an officer's name | | Do not know an officer's name | |
|---|---|---|---|---|
| 34th Residents | 7% | (2) | 93% | (28) |
| 114th Residents | 0 | (0) | 100 | (14) |
| 34th Businessmen | 20 | (8) | 80 | (32) |
| 114th Businessmen | 5 | (1) | 95 | (19) |
| 34th Youth | 40 | (12) | 60 | (18) |
| 114th Youth | 35 | (7) | 65 | (13) |
| 34th Community Meeting Participants | 68 | (17) | 32 | (8) |

Citizens who had heard of Operation Neighborhood were asked if they
thought that the program had had any effect in their neighborhood. As Table
49 shows they tended to believe that it had not.

TABLE 49: CITIZEN ESTIMATE OF OPERATION NEIGHBORHOOD'S EFFECT
(Percent, followed by absolute numbers in parentheses)

Citizens who had heard of the program were asked: Do you think Operation
Neighborhood has had any effect in your neighborhood?

| Respondent Group (Operation Neighborhood only) | Some effect on Neighborhood | | No effect on Neighborhood | |
|---|---|---|---|---|
| Residents | 40% | (4) | 60% | (6) |
| Businessmen | 56 | (15) | 44 | (12) |
| Youth | 38 | (3) | 62 | (5) |
| Community Meeting Participants | 25 | (6) | 75 | (18) |

Nevertheless, the citizens indicated confidence in the program. Those who had heard of Operation Neighborhood believed that the program would have an important effect if it was continued over an extended period of time. (See Table 50.)

TABLE 50: CITIZEN ESTIMATE OF OPERATION NEIGHBORHOOD'S FUTURE IMPACT
(Percent, followed by absolute numbers in parentheses)

Do you think if Operation Neighborhood is in your area for an extended period of time that it might have an important effect here?

| GROUP | Will have an effect over time | | Will not have an effect over time | |
|---|---|---|---|---|
| Residents | 80% | (8) | 20% | (2) |
| Businessmen | 89 | (24) | 11 | (3) |
| Youth | 67 | (6) | 33 | (3) |
| Community Meeting Participants | 88 | (21) | 12 | (3) |

NOTE: This question was asked only of residents in Operation Neighborhood areas who had heard of the program.

In one respect, Operation Neighborhood seems to have had a small effect. Citizens in the 34th Precinct, when compared to citizens in the 114th Precinct, were more likely to say they had seen policemen doing something that pleased them. (See Table 51.) They mentioned two principal reasons for being pleased with police behavior: (1) the police seemed to patrol more often and (2) the police seemed to respond to calls more quickly. The reasons given by citizens in the 114th Precinct were similar.

TABLE 51:   PERCENT OF CITIZENS PLEASED WITH SOME POLICE ACTION

Have you seen the police doing anything in this neighborhood which makes you pleased that they are working here?

| GROUP | YES | NO |
|---|---|---|
| 34th Residents | 47% | 53% |
| 114th Residents | 36 | 64 |
| 34th Businessmen | 70 | 30 |
| 114th Businessmen | 50 | 50 |
| 34th Youth | 20 | 80 |
| 114th Youth | 15 | 85 |
| 34th Community Meeting Participants | 68 | 32 |

Citizens in the 34th Precinct were also a little more likely to report that, compared to a year ago, the police were on foot patrol more often. (See Table 52.)

TABLE 52:   CITIZEN PERCEPTION OF FREQUENCY OF FOOT PATROL

Compared to a year ago, how often would you say that patrolmen were on foot in the neighborhood?

| ALTERNATIVE | RESIDENTS 34th Precinct | RESIDENTS 114th Precinct | BUSINESSMEN 34th Precinct | BUSINESSMEN 114th Precinct | YOUTH 34th Precinct | YOUTH 114th Precinct | COMMUNITY MEETING PARTICIPANTS 34th Precinct |
|---|---|---|---|---|---|---|---|
| Much more often | 7% | 0% | 18% | 5% | 20% | 10% | 4% |
| A little more often | 23 | 0 | 28 | 25 | 3 | 10 | 20 |
| About as often | 63 | 100 | 50 | 45 | 27 | 55 | 52 |
| A little less often | 7 | 0 | 5 | 20 | 0 | 5 | 16 |
| Much less | 0 | 0 | 0 | 5 | 50 | 20 | 8 |

Nevertheless, Operation Neighborhood apparently had little effect on an individual's feeling that he was safer from crime.  (See Tables 53, 54, and 55.)

TABLE 53:   CITIZEN FEELINGS OF SAFETY COMPARED WITH A YEAR AGO

Compared to a year ago, how safe do you think you are walking alone in this neighborhood at night?

| ALTERNATIVE | RESIDENTS | | BUSINESSMEN | | YOUTH | | COMMUNITY MEETING PARTICIPANTS 34th Precinct |
|---|---|---|---|---|---|---|---|
| | 34th Precinct | 114th Precinct | 34th Precinct | 114th Precinct | 34th Precinct | 114th Precinct | |
| Much safer | 0% | 0% | 5% | 10% | 0% | 10% | 4% |
| A little safer | 3 | 0 | 3 | 15 | 10 | 5 | 16 |
| About as safe | 47 | 43 | 55 | 20 | 40 | 15 | 44 |
| A little less safe | 27 | 28 | 28 | 10 | 17 | 25 | 24 |
| Much less safe | 23 | 28 | 10 | 45 | 33 | 45 | 12 |
| MEAN | 3.70 | 3.96 | 3.35 | 3.65 | 3.73 | 3.90 | 3.24 |

TABLE 54:   CITIZEN FEELINGS OF SAFETY COMPARED WITH
PREVIOUS YEAR--34TH PRECINCT

When you think of crime in this neighborhood, <u>compared to last year</u>, do you think that you are. . .

Alternatives (in percent)

| GROUP | Much Safer | A Little Safer | About As Safe | A Little Less Safe | Much Less Safe | MEAN |
|---|---|---|---|---|---|---|
| RESIDENTS | | | | | | |
|   Have heard of NPT | 0% | 10% | 60% | 30% | 0% | 3.20 |
|   Have not heard of NPT | 0 | 0 | 35 | 40 | 25 | 3.90 |
| BUSINESSMEN | | | | | | |
|   Have heard of NPT | 4 | 7 | 56 | 26 | 7 | 3.26 |
|   Have not heard of NPT | 15 | 0 | 62 | 8 | 15 | 3.08 |
| YOUTH | | | | | | |
|   Have heard of NPT | 0 | 22 | 33 | 22 | 22 | 3.44 |
|   Have not heard of NPT | 15 | 33 | 33 | 14 | 14 | 3.00 |
| COMMUNITY MEETING PARTICIPANTS | | | | | | |
|   Have heard of NPT* | 0 | 17 | 42 | 25 | 17 | 3.42 |

*Only one had not heard of the program.

TABLE 55:   BELIEF IN SAFETY OF A WOMAN WALKING ALONE

<u>Compared to a year ago,</u> how safe do you think a young woman is walking alone in this neighborhood?

Alternatives (in percent)

| GROUP | Much Safer | A Little Safer | About As Safe | A Little Less Safe | Much Less Safe | MEAN |
|---|---|---|---|---|---|---|
| RESIDENTS | | | | | | |
| Have heard of NPT | 0% | 0% | 50% | 30% | 20 % | 3.70 |
| Have not heard of NPT | 0 | 5 | 45 | 25 | 25 | 3.70 |
| BUSINESSMEN | | | | | | |
| Have heard of NPT | 0 | 4 | 52 | 33 | 11 | 3.52 |
| Have not heard of NPT | 15 | 0 | 62 | 15 | 8 | 3.00 |
| YOUTH | | | | | | |
| Have heard of NPT | * | * | * | * | * | * |
| Have not heard of NPT | | | | | | |
| COMMUNITY MEETING PARTICIPANTS | | | | | | |
| Have heard of NPT** | 4 | 17 | 42 | 25 | 13 | 3.17 |

*All of the respondents in the Youth Category were young women. This question was not asked of this group because they had already been asked whether they felt safe in their neighborhood.
**Only one had not heard of the program.

Citizen views on police corruption were also explored in the survey. Surprisingly, quite a few respondents chose not to answer the question concerning the effect of payoffs. (See Table 56.) The form of the question, rather than the subject matter, may have been the influencing factor.

Citizens who did answer the question tended to believe that police effectiveness was decreased as a result of police corruption. While there was little difference on this question between precincts, caution should be used in interpreting the results.

TABLE 56:   EFFECT OF PAYOFFS ON CRIME CONTROL

Some people say that police take payoffs and that makes it difficult to control crime.

| RESPONSE (Do You—) | RESIDENTS 34th[a] Precinct | 114th Precinct | BUSINESSMEN 34th[b] Precinct | 114th Precinct | YOUTH 34th[c] Precinct | 114th Precinct | COMMUNITY MEETING PARTICIPANTS[d] 34th Precinct |
|---|---|---|---|---|---|---|---|
| Strongly agree | 12 % | 62 % | 13 % | 19 % | 54 % | 63 % | 14% |
| Agree | 77 | 31 | 70 | 38 | 21 | 21 | 82 |
| Mildly agree | 4 | 0 | 0 | 6 | 14 | 0 | 0 |
| Disagree | 0 | 8 | 3 | 32 | 11 | 11 | 5 |
| Strongly disagree | 8 | 0 | 13 | 6 | 0 | 5 | 0 |

[a]Only 26 residents in the 34th and 13 residents in the 114th answered this question.

[b]Only 30 businessmen in the 34th and 16 businessmen in the 114th answered this question.

[c]Only 28 youths in the 34th and 19 youths in the 114th answered this question.

[d]Only 22 community meeting participants answered this question.

THE PATROL OFFICER'S PERCEPTIONS OF CITIZEN SUPPORT

A number of patrol survey questions concerning citizen support were used to formulate an Index of General Citizen Support.[15]  The results show that Precinct 34 has a higher score than does Precinct 79.  This indicates that police in Precinct 34 perceive more citizen support than do police in Precinct 79.  The volunteer group showed a decline on this index from April to June.  Otherwise, there is little difference between the Operation Neighborhood groups and the comparison groups.  (See Tables 57 and 58.)

---

15.   See Appendix C for an explanation of how the various indexes were constructed.

TABLE 57:   INDEX OF POLICE VIEWS ON GENERAL CITIZEN SUPPORT--RAW SCORES

| OPERATION NEIGHBORHOOD | | COMPARISON GROUPS | |
|---|---|---|---|
| | June | | June |
| Volunteers | 123.3 | Comparisons | 122.7 |
| Precinct 6 | 123.6 | Precinct 114 | 123.3 |
| Precinct 34 | 126.4 | Precinct 79 | 119.5 |
| Precinct 24 | 121.7 | | |

TABLE 58:   INDEX OF POLICE VIEWS ON GENERAL CITIZEN SUPPORT--ADJUSTED SCORES

| OPERATION NEIGHBORHOOD | | | | | COMPARSION GROUPS | |
|---|---|---|---|---|---|---|
| | Overall Mean | Jan. | April | June | | Overall Mean |
| Volunteers | 120.5 | 120.1 | 121.6 | 119.3 | Comparison Groups and Precinct 114 | 120.2 |
| Precinct 6 | 121.3 | | | | | |
| Precinct 34 | 122.6 | | | | Precinct 79 | 118.7 |
| Precinct 24 | 119.4 | | | | | |

When asked about the number of compliments they had received from citizens in the last month, patrolmen in Operation Neighborhood groups reported more compliments than did patrolmen in the comparison groups. As indicated on Table 59, the greatest differences are between the scores of all comparison groups combined and Precincts 34 and 6.

TABLE 59:   NUMBER OF COMPLIMENTS PATROLMEN RECEIVED
FROM CITIZENS IN LAST MONTH
(Adjusted for Seniority of Three Years or Less)

| OPERATION NEIGHBORHOOD | | COMPARISON GROUPS | |
|---|---|---|---|
| | Overall Mean | | Overall Mean |
| Volunteers | 4.85 | All Comparison Groups Combined | 3.15 |
| Precinct 6 | 5.38 | | |
| Precinct 34 | 6.15 | | |
| Precinct 24 | 3.33 | | |

Police views on various types of citizen support were explored in the survey. Precinct 34 patrolmen expressed the most confidence in the likelihood that a citizen would call for assistance if he saw a policeman in trouble. (See Table 60.) Precinct 114 patrolmen reported a relatively small likelihood of citizen help during the June wave. In fact, the difference between the April and the June waves showed a significant deterioration.

TABLE 60: ESTIMATE OF CITIZEN WILLINGNESS TO HELP A POLICEMAN IN TROUBLE
(Adjusted for the Log of Seniority)

How often do people help by calling for assistance when they see that a policeman is in trouble?

1. Almost never  2. Seldom  3. Sometimes  4. Often  5. Almost always

| OPERATION NEIGHBORHOOD | | COMPARISON GROUPS | | | | |
|---|---|---|---|---|---|---|
| | Overall Mean | | Overall Mean | Jan. | April | June |
| Volunteers | 3.70 | Precinct 114 | 3.68 | 3.60 | 4.07 | 3.26 |
| Precinct 6 | 3.52 | Comparisons and | | | | |
| Precinct 34 | 4.09 | Precinct 79 | 3.60 | | | |
| Precinct 24 | 3.53 | | | | | |

TABLE 61: ESTIMATE OF CITIZEN WILLINGNESS TO HELP
WRONGFULLY-ACCUSED POLICEMAN WITH TESTIMONY
(Adjusted for the Log of Seniority)*

How often will people volunteer or agree to testify in a policeman's behalf if they know that he has been unjustifiably accused of misconduct?

1. Almost never  2. Seldom  3. Sometimes  4. Often  5. Almost always

| OPERATION NEIGHBORHOOD | | | | | COMPARISON GROUPS | |
|---|---|---|---|---|---|---|
| | Overall Mean | Jan. | April | June | | Overall Mean |
| Volunteers | 2.27 | | | | All Comparison | |
| Precinct 6 | 2.25 | | | | Groups Combined | 2.04 |
| Precinct 34 | 2.35 | 2.29 | 2.04 | 2.80 | | |
| Precinct 24 | 1.78 | | | | | |

*Apparently seniority is a strong positive factor. Officers with longer service expect more citizen support in this respect.

Patrolmen were asked to estimate the proportion of people in their precinct who belonged to groups that supported the police, politically or otherwise. Little difference was found among the groups except that the estimates of the volunteers and Precinct 24 patrolmen tended to be lower. (See Table 62.) In April, the volunteers reported a larger percent of people belonging to such groups than they did in June.

TABLE 62: PATROLMAN'S ESTIMATE OF PERCENT OF PEOPLE
IN GROUPS SUPPORTING THE POLICE
(Adjusted for the Log of Seniority)

What percent of the people in your precinct belong to groups which support the police politically or as volunteers?

| OPERATION NEIGHBORHOOD | | | | | COMPARISON GROUPS | |
|---|---|---|---|---|---|---|
| | Overall Mean | Jan. | April | June | | Overall Mean |
| Volunteers | 13.9 | 10.6 | 20.0 | 9.0 | Precinct 79 | 19.2 |
| Precinct 6 | 21.0 | | | | All Comparisons and Precinct 114 | 15.4 |
| Precinct 34 | 21.2 | | | | | |
| Precinct 24 | 14.5 | | | | | |

Similar results were found when the police were asked to estimate how much they were appreciated by the public. In April, the volunteers reported a higher estimate than they did in June. (See Table 63.)

TABLE 63: PATROLMAN'S ESTIMATE OF PUBLIC APPRECIATION
(Adjusted for the Log of Seniority)

Choose one of the following sets of characteristics which gives your individual impressions of your job during the last month.

1. Looked down on by the public  2. Not appreciated by the public  3. Mildly appreciated by the public  4. Appreciated by the public  5. Greatly appreciated by the public

| OPERATION NEIGHBORHOOD | | | | | COMPARISON GROUPS | | | | |
|---|---|---|---|---|---|---|---|---|---|
| | Overall Mean | Jan. | April | June | | Overall Mean | Jan. | April | June |
| Volunteers | 2.63 | 2.36 | 2.97 | 2.46 | Comparisons | 2.75 | | | |
| Precinct 6 | 2.63 | | | | Precinct 114 | 2.38 | | | |
| Precinct 34 | 2.68 | | | | Precinct 79 | 2.49 | | 2.73 | 2.20 |
| Precinct 24 | 2.42 | | | | | | | | |

WRITTEN COMPLAINTS AND COMMENDATIONS FROM THE PUBLIC

As part of this evaluation, the written communications of one Operation Neighborhood precinct were studied. The intention was to compare communications (especially complaints and commendations) before and after Operation Nieghborhood guidelines were promulgated.[16] Table 64 gives a breakdown of the communications handled in Precinct 34 during two such periods.[17]

TABLE 64:  COMPARISON OF THE NUMBER AND TYPE OF COMMUNICATIONS IN PRECINCT 34 BEFORE AND AFTER IMPLEMENTATION OF OPERATION NEIGHBORHOOD

| Type of Communication | January-May 1971 Before Operation Neighborhood | January-May 1972 After Implementation of Operation Neighborhood |
|---|---|---|
| Citizen Commendations | 24 | 56 |
| Citizen Complaints | 126 | 91 |
| Police Department Communications | 120 | 203* |
| Other Agencies-- Complaints or Communications | 76 | 99* |
| TOTAL | 346 | 449 |

*The large increase in the number of communications from within the department and other agencies reflects the many procedural and organizational changes that were made during the start up period and the inter-departmental orders that were issued.

Significant changes are evident in the number and types of communications handled in Precinct 34. Under Operation Neighborhood, the number of citizen complaints (involving such items as noise, parking conditions, failure of police to deal with a problem, etc.) decreased from 126 to 91. It is perhaps more important, however, that the number of commendations from citizens for good police service more than doubled under Operation Neighborhood. The increase was from 24 to 56 commendations.

16.  T.O.P. 364, January 1, 1971.  See Appendix A, page 127.
17.  Although the precinct did not handle or record communications concerning gambling, public morals, vice or corruption beginning in January 1972, very few of the communications received in January-May 1971 involved these areas.

The reduction in complaints and increase in commendations may indicate that Operation Neighborhood has had a significant effect on increasing the quality of police service. However, neighborhood teams may also have had an effect by handling more complaints informally, before they became written communications, and by encouraging citizens to submit letters of commendation.

Earlier, a study was made of civilian complaints in Precinct 34 and in the areas served by volunteer teams.[18] The results from the January through December 1971 period showed that patrolmen on nine neighborhood teams received fewer complaints per man (.14 per man/year) than non-team patrolmen in the same precincts (.23 per man/year). However, the number of civilian complaints against Precinct 34 police for September 1971 through January 1972 (under Operation Neighborhood) was double the number for September 1970 through January 1971 (before Operation Neighborhood). This increase in civilian complaints may have been due to the initial increased visibility and activity of Precinct 34 patrolmen. In any case, it did not last.

---

18. Bloch and Specht, op. cit.

## IX

## POLICE ATTITUDES TOWARD CORRUPTION

In the order establishing Operation Neighborhood, Chief Inspector
Michael J. Codd made this comment on one detrimental effect of departmental
efforts to control police corruption: *"For many years our operation procedures have placed a main emphasis on the prevention of misconduct and many
of the restrictive features of this emphasis have had a detrimental effect
on police-public relations."* He went on to say: *"While misconduct will
continue to be fought with every means possible, the main emphasis of our
operating procedures will now be service to the public."*[19]

Unfortunately, corruption must still be considered a live issue in the
New York City Police Department. The Knapp Commission's findings, which
were headlined in most of the city's newspapers, had a profound effect on the
whole department.

The opportunity for corruption in areas served by neighborhood police
teams caused some concern. On the one hand, greater police-citizen contact
would result in more temptations. On the other hand, it was hoped that
corruption might be reduced (a) by bringing police attitudes closer to community attitudes and (b) by holding a sergeant responsible for an area.

One team commander expressed the following views on the subject in his
September report:

> *The potential of corruption of team members is lessened by the
> fact that these men are, for the most part, picked volunteers, whose
> job attitude and morals are above average. The fact that these men
> are known by the people residing and doing business in the area, in
> which they are assigned, serves as a reminder to them that they may
> well be questioned as to their actions in any given situation.*

---

19. T.O.P. December 30, 1970. See Appendix A, page 127.

Two questions in the patrol survey were concerned with bribes. Patrolmen were asked to estimate the percent of businessmen in the precinct who were willing to offer a tip or a meal. In addition, they were asked to report how many individuals indicated an interest in an exchange of favors. Before discussing the results, some important factors must be considered.

There is a natural reluctance among police to admit that corruption is a problem within the department. The more conservative and older patrolmen are less likely to reveal the temptations toward corruption. Nevertheless, a greater willingness to disclose such temptations is considered a development in the right direction. Hopefully, this openness would be accompanied by a decline in the number of bribes offered to police. Over time as they learned that bribes would not be accepted, citizens would either stop making such offers or at least make them less often.

No significant differences between Operation Neighborhood groups and the comparison groups appear on the "Index of Citizen Willingness to Tempt Policemen with Favors." Although not statistically significant, there is a promising trend in Precinct 34, which shows increases on this index (i.e., less corruption) in each successive wave of interviews. (See Tables 65, 66 and 67.)

TABLE 65: INDEX OF CITIZEN WILLINGNESS TO TEMPT POLICEMEN
WITH FAVORS--ADJUSTED SCORES*
(Adjusted for Seniority of the Patrolmen)

| OPERATION NEIGHBORHOOD | | COMPARISON GROUPS | |
|---|---|---|---|
| | Mean | | Mean |
| Volunteers | 99.4 | Precinct 79 | 101.0 |
| Precinct 6 | 99.8 | Comparisons and Precinct 114 | 97.1 |
| Precinct 34 | 97.3 | | |
| Precinct 24 | 96.3 | | |

*A higher index score indicates a perception of less corruption.

TABLE 66:   INDEX OF CITIZEN WILLINGNESS TO TEMPT POLICEMEN
WITH FAVORS--RAW SCORES

| OPERATION NEIGHBORHOOD | | COMPARISON GROUPS | |
|---|---|---|---|
| | June | | June |
| Volunteers | 100.8 | Comparisons | 98.6 |
| Precinct 6 | 100.9 | Precinct 114 | 100.9 |
| Precinct 34 | 94.6 | Precinct 79 | 102.1 |
| Precinct 24 | 97.4 | | |

Standard Deviation = 12.4

TABLE 67:   PATROLMAN'S ESTIMATE OF PRECINCT BUSINESSMEN
WILLING TO OFFER A BRIBE

(Adjusted for Seniority of Patrolmen)

In the last month, about what percent of businessmen in the precinct would have liked to give a policeman a meal or small tip because they want him to be friendly and to be sympathetic if they should have a problem in the future?

| OPERATION NEIGHBORHOOD | | | COMPARISON GROUPS | | |
|---|---|---|---|---|---|
| | January | April-June | | January | April-June |
| Volunteers | 12.7% | 5.6% | All Comparison Groups Combined | 17.4% | 10.3% |
| Precinct 6 | | 9.3 | | | |
| Precinct 34 | | 9.6 | | | |
| Precinct 24 | 17.4 | 10.8 | | | |

In the January wave, volunteers reported a lower percentage of business-men willing to offer a meal or small tip than did all comparison groups combined.  (See Table 67.)

The department, as a whole, reported a decrease in the percentage of businessmen who would offer a tip or meal from January to June.  This decrease may be attributed (a) to the influence of the Knapp Commission's hearings and (b) to the department's publicized efforts to prosecute any individuals caught offering bribes.

There were no significant differences between Operation Neighborhood and comparison groups on the question of businessmen doing a favor for a policeman in return for special consideration.

X

CITIZEN HOSTILITY TOWARD POLICE

In theory, police relations with a community are a simple, two-sided affair. But in fact, the police frequently find that a community is composed of diverse elements, each requiring a certain approach. One group of citizens may provide active support by supplying information to the police about crime. Another group of citizens may be only generally supportive or neutral towards the police. Yet another important group of citizens may be hostile toward the police, i.e., a potential force of opposition and injury.

Because of the deep roots of citizen hostility in many communities, it will be most difficult to influence some people's attitudes. Indeed, our survey showed that neighborhood police teams had little success in reaching hostile citizens. The only significant difference was that Precinct 6 patrolmen reported a more hostile community than did other patrolmen in the study. (See Tables 68 and 69.) This hostility is reflected in a number of ways. Precinct 6 patrolmen report that, on average, people either threatened

TABLE 68:  INDEX OF CITIZEN HOSTILITY--ADJUSTED SCORES
(Adjusted for Seniority of Patrolmen)*

| OPERATION NEIGHBORHOOD | | COMPARISON GROUPS | |
|---|---|---|---|
| | Overall Mean | | Overall Mean |
| Volunteers | 88.9 | All Comparison Groups Combined | 88.6 |
| Precinct 6 | 81.9 | | |
| Precinct 34 | 91.0 | | |
| Precinct 24 | 86.8 | | |

*High index scores show less hostility. Seniority has a strong effect. Older patrolmen perceive less citizen hostility.

TABLE 69:  INDEX OF CITIZENS HOSTILITY--RAW SCORES

| OPERATION NEIGHBORHOOD | | COMPARISON GROUPS | |
|---|---|---|---|
| | June | | June |
| Volunteers | 89.5 | Comparisons | 91.7 |
| Precinct 6 | 84.5 | Precinct 114 | 95.6 |
| Precinct 34 | 99.2 | Precinct 79 | 83.8 |
| Precinct 24 | 88.9 | | |

or attempted to injure them over 2.6 times in the last month.  This is a significantly higher number than was reported by any of the other groups. (See Table 70.)

TABLE 70:  NUMBER OF TIMES CITIZENS THREATENED OR
ATTEMPTED TO INJURE PATROLMAN IN LAST MONTH
(Adjusted for Seniority of the Patrolman)

About how many times have people threatened or attempted to injure you in the last month?

| | Mean | Standard Error |
|---|---|---|
| Precinct 6 (Operation Neighborhood) | 2.66 | 4.30 |
| Precinct 24 (Operation Neighborhood) | 2.17 | 4.18 |
| Precinct 79 (Comparison Group) | 2.17 | 3.45 |
| All Other Groups (Volunteers, Precincts 34 and 114) | 1.86 | 1.96 |

Precinct 6 stands out in a similar fashion on a related question.  In response to an inquiry about the attitude of bystanders witnessing an arrest after dark, Precinct 6 patrolmen report that over 38 percent of the bystanders would like to see them physically harmed.  (See Table 71.)  Precinct 34 patrolmen, on the other hand, report that only 19 percent of the bystanders would like to see them physically harmed.  This estimate is significantly lower than that registered by all comparison groups combined.

TABLE 71:  PERCENT OF BYSTANDERS WISHING POLICE WOULD BE HARMED

What percentage of bystanders do you think would like you to be physically harmed when you make an arrest on the street after dark in your
precinct?

| OPERATION NEIGHBORHOOD | | | | COMPARISON GROUPS | | | |
|---|---|---|---|---|---|---|---|
| | January | April | June | | January | April | June |
| Volunteers | 32.2 | 28.1 | 26.2 | All Comparison Groups Combined | 32.1 | 28.0 | 26.1 |
| Precinct 6 | | | 38.2 | | | | |
| Precinct 34 | 25.0 | 20.9 | 19.0 | | | | |
| Precinct 24 | | | 29.1 | | | | |

Following the trend already established, Precinct 6 patrolmen also
reported a larger percentage of citizens belonging to groups that oppose
police.  (See Table 72.)  Comparing bystander hostility at the time of the
survey to bystander hostility a year ago, Precinct 6 patrolmen reported more
of a change for the worse than all the others.  (See Table 73.)  The difference on this question is not statistically important.  What is important,
however, is a trend in the responses to questions grouped for the Index of
Citizen Hostility.  The trend indicates that policemen perceive the community
as increasingly hostile.

TABLE 72:  PATROLMAN'S ESTIMATE OF THE PERCENT OF CITIZENS
BELONGING TO GROUPS WHICH OPPOSE POLICE
(Adjusted for the Log of a Patrolman's Seniority)

What percent of the people in your precinct belong to groups which
regularly oppose police?

| OPERATION NEIGHBORHOOD | | COMPARISON GROUPS | |
|---|---|---|---|
| | Overall Mean | | Overall Mean |
| Precinct 6 | 38.1 | Precinct 79 | 18.6 |
| Precinct 34 | 12.4 | Comparisons and Precinct 114 | 15.7 |
| Precinct 24 | 20.0 | | |

TABLE 73: COMPARISON OF BYSTANDER HOSTILITY TOWARDS POLICE
LAST MONTH VS. LAST YEAR

When you have responded to a public argument or street fight <u>during the last month</u>, was bystander hostility <u>compared to a year ago</u> getting:

1. Much Worse   2. A little   3. About the   4. A little   5. Much better
           worse       same        better

| OPERATION NEIGHBORHOOD | | COMPARISON GROUPS | |
|---|---|---|---|
| | Overall Mean | | Overall Mean |
| Volunteers | 2.40 | All Comparison Groups Combined | 2.54 |
| Precinct 6 | 2.23 | | |
| Precinct 34 | 2.54 | | |
| Precinct 24 | 2.39 | | |

No significant differences among groups are evident in their estimate of the danger associated with policing. However, it is interesting to note that there was a decrease in the score of Precinct 34 from April to June. (See Table 74.)

TABLE 74: PATROLMAN'S ESTIMATE OF DANGER INHERENT IN POLICING

Choose one of the following sets of characteristics which gives your <u>individual impressions</u> of your job <u>during the last month</u>:

1. A little   2. Quite risky   3. Pretty      4. Very       5. Extremely
   risky                     dangerous     dangerous     dangerous

| OPERATION NEIGHBORHOOD | | | | | COMPARISON GROUPS | |
|---|---|---|---|---|---|---|
| | Overall Mean | Jan. | April | June | | Overall Mean |
| Volunteers | 3.66 | | | | All Comparison Groups Combined | 3.60 |
| Precinct 6 | 3.00 | | | 3.00 | | |
| Precinct 34 | 3.77 | 3.70 | 4.30 | 3.28 | | |
| Precinct 24 | 3.84 | | | 3.84 | | |

XI

SATISFACTION WITH THE POLICING PROFESSION

As stated earlier, Operation Neighborhood intended to involve the patrolman in shaping the policy of his police team. It also hoped to interest him in a variety of patrol techniques which would be more rewarding than the routine procedures formerly used. Once these goals were achieved, it was believed (a) that there would be a greater exchange of information among policemen and (b) that more reasonable team policies would be developed. Thus it was hoped that the police would be more satisfied with their jobs and less likely to be irritated or provoked to violence.

## OPEN-ENDED QUESTIONS

One way to test whether patrolmen in Operation Neighborhood are in fact becoming more satisfied with their jobs is to ask them whether their jobs are getting better or worse. The answers to this question reveal that 80 percent of the respondents in Operation Neighborhood teams believe their job is getting worse. While the morale of these patrolmen may be higher than it is in the rest of our sample (90 percent of whom believe their job is getting worse, see Table 75), the low degree of job satisfaction is hardly a hearty endorsement for Operation Neighborhood. In addition, we asked the patrolmen what they thought should be done to improve the patrol division. Only a scant percentage of officers in Operation Neighborhood suggested that the expansion of the program would represent an improvement in the department. No one outside of the program thought to mention Operation Neighborhood as a way of improving the department (see Table 76).

TABLE 75: PATROLMAN'S EXPECTATIONS ABOUT JOB

(JUNE RESULTS)

| | JOB GETTING BETTER | | | | WORSE | | No Response | TOTAL |
|---|---|---|---|---|---|---|---|---|
| | Job Reasons* | Pay, Fringes | Total | | | | | |
| | # | # | # | % | # | % | # | # |
| Precinct 6 | $3\frac{1}{2}$** | 0 | $3\frac{1}{2}$ | 21.9 | $10\frac{1}{2}$ | 65.6 | 2 | 16 |
| Precinct 24 | 2 | 1 | 3 | 20.0 | 8 | 53.3 | 4 | 15 |
| Precinct 34 | 3 | 0 | 3 | 18.6 | 12 | 75.0 | 1 | 16 |
| Volunteer Neighborhood | $2\frac{1}{2}$ | 0 | $2\frac{1}{2}$ | 13.2 | $11\frac{1}{2}$ | 60.5 | 5 | 19 |
| Total Operation Neighborhood | 11 | 1 | 12 | 18.2 | 42 | 63.6 | 12 | 66 |
| Precinct 79 | 1 | $\frac{1}{2}$ | $1\frac{1}{2}$ | 11.5 | $8\frac{1}{2}$ | 65.4 | 3 | 13 |
| Precinct 114 | 1 | 0 | 1 | 7.7 | 9 | 69.2 | 3 | 13 |
| Comparisons | 1 | 0 | 1 | 7.1 | 10 | 71.4 | 3 | 14 |
| Total Comparison Groups | 1 | $\frac{1}{2}$ | $3\frac{1}{2}$ | 8.8 | $27\frac{1}{2}$ | 68.8 | 9 | 40 |

*"Job Reasons" includes any statement about the community or the job other than pay.

**"$\frac{1}{2}$" indicates that a patrolman gave an answer which had both positive and negative statements about his job.

TABLE 76: PATROLMAN'S SUGGESTIONS FOR IMPROVING THE PATROL FORCE

| | # Completed Question | Extend Operation Neighborhood | More Men | More Community Relations | More Foot Patrol or Scooter | Get Tougher | Better Supervision | Training in Law | Incentives for Arrests | More Plainclothes | Improve Salary | Experiment | Reduce Paperwork | Emphasize Patrol Activity | Reduce Unimportant Runs | Other |
|---|---|---|---|---|---|---|---|---|---|---|---|---|---|---|---|---|
| 6th Precinct | 16 | 0 | 6.3 | 0 | 12.5 | 0 | 18.8 | 0 | 12.5 | 12.5 | 0 | 0 | 12.5 | 37.5 | 31.3 | 18.8 |
| 24th Precinct | 13 | 0 | 0 | 7.7 | 0 | 0 | 15.4 | 7.7 | 15.4 | 0 | 7.7 | 0 | 7.7 | 38.5 | 15.4 | 38.5 |
| 34th Precinct | 17 | 0 | 17.6 | 17.6 | 17.6 | 23.5 | 17.6 | 5.9 | 11.8 | 23.5 | 0 | 0 | 5.9 | 5.9 | 23.5 | 41.2 |
| Volunteers | 14 | 7.1 | 7.1 | 14.3 | 7.1 | 7.1 | 7.1 | 14.3 | 7.1 | 28.6 | 7.1 | 0 | 35.7 | 7.1 | 21.4 | 21.4 |
| Total Operation Neighborhood | 60 | 1.7 | 8.3 | 10.0 | 11.7 | 8.3 | 15.0 | 6.7 | 11.7 | 16.7 | 3.3 | 0 | 15.0 | 21.7 | 20.0 | 30.0 |
| 79th Precinct | 7 | 0 | 28.6 | 0 | 14.3 | 0 | 42.9 | 0 | 28.6 | 0 | 0 | 0 | 0 | 14.3 | 14.3 | 71.4 |
| 114th Precinct | 10 | 0 | 20.0 | 0 | 0 | 10.0 | 0 | 10.0 | 10.0 | 20.0 | 0 | 0 | 0 | 20.0 | 40.0 | 30.0 |
| Comparisons | 10 | 0 | 30.0 | 0 | 40.0 | 0 | 30.0 | 10.0 | 40.0 | 40.0 | 10.0 | 0 | 20.0 | 0 | 0 | 50.0 |
| Total Comparison Groups | 27 | 0 | 25.9 | 0 | 18.5 | 3.7 | 22.2 | 7.4 | 25.9 | 22.2 | 3.7 | 0 | 7.4 | 11.1 | 18.5 | 48.1 |

NOTE: Table entries are percentages of respondents unless otherwise indicated.

A patrolman's belief that his job is getting better or worse may be highly influenced by events that have nothing to do with Operation Neighborhood. In this instance, it may well be that the many operational changes-- some of which were designed to reduce corruption in the police force--were so highly resented by the men that the implementation of the Operation Neighborhood Program had a greatly diminished effect. Under other conditions, it may be that Operation Neighborhood would have resulted in greater job satisfaction.

## INDEX OF SATISFACTION WITH THE POLICING PROFESSION

Included in the patrol survey were several questions designed to determine whether Operation Neighborhood had improved a patrolman's satisfaction with the policing profession. While it appears that Operation Neighborhood had no important effect, seniority did have an effect. It seems that men with less seniority are more likely to be satisfied with their jobs as policemen than are men with more seniority. (See Tables 77 and 78.)

TABLE 77: INDEX OF SATISFACTION WITH THE POLICING PROFESSION
ADJUSTED SCORES (Corrected for Seniority of the Patrolmen)

| OPERATION NEIGHBORHOOD | | COMPARISON GROUPS | |
|---|---|---|---|
| | Mean | | Mean |
| Volunteers | 104.6 | All Comparison Groups Combined | 102.8 |
| Precinct 6 | 106.7 | | |
| Precinct 34 | 104.6 | | |
| Precinct 24 | 108.2 | | |

TABLE 78:   INDEX OF SATISFACTION WITH THE POLICING PROFESSION
(RAW SCORES)

| OPERATION NEIGHBORHOOD | | COMPARISON GROUPS | |
|---|---|---|---|
| | June | | June |
| Volunteers | 98.4 | Comparisons | 96.3 |
| Precinct 6 | 97.8 | Precinct 114 | 95.8 |
| Precinct 34 | 100.2 | Precinct 79 | 96.4 |
| Precinct 24 | 99.6 | | |

Standard Deviation = 5.39

On one important question within this index, some Operation Neighborhood groups report greater job satisfaction. Patrolmen in Precinct 34, comparison Precinct 79 and Precinct 24 all reported that in the last month their job activities were more satisfying than did the comparisons and Precinct 114 combined. (See Table 79.)

TABLE 79:   FREQUENCY OF PATROLMAN'S SATISFACTION WITH JOB ACTIVITIES
(Adjusted for the Log of Patrolman's Seniority)

How often in the last month have your job activities given you satisfaction?

1.  Almost never  2.  Seldom  3.  Sometimes  4.  Often  5.  Almost always

| OPERATION NEIGHBORHOOD | | COMPARISON GROUPS | |
|---|---|---|---|
| | Overall Mean | | Overall Mean |
| Volunteers | 3.26 | Precinct 79 | 3.67 |
| Precinct 6 | 3.24 | Comparison Groups and Precinct 114 | 3.13 |
| Precinct 34 | 3.54 | | |
| Precinct 24 | 3.55 | | |

## OTHER FACTORS RELATED TO JOB SATISFACTION

Many of the factors influencing a patrolman's interest in his job are subjective; others are objective. Two of the most important ones concern the patrolman's usefulness to the public and the amount of discretion he is allowed to exercise. Operation Neighborhood guidelines directed officials to encourage patrolmen to think about and discuss their job. It was hoped that by forming their own opinions and making suggestions, team members would recognize that their task is extremely complex and that it requires a considerable amount of discretion and judgment. As Table 80 indicates, Operation Neighborhood groups did report that they used discretion or their own judgment more often than did the comparison groups.

TABLE 80:  REPORTED USE OF DISCRETION AND JUDGMENT
(Adjusted for the Log of the Patrolmen's Seniority)

When you respond to a situation, how much of what you do is the result of your own judgment or discretion (as opposed to just following orders or doing what the law requires)?

1. Almost no discretion or judgment used    2. Some discretion or judgment    3. Often use discretion or judgment    4. Almost always use discretion or judgment

| OPERATION NEIGHBORHOOD | | | | | COMPARISON GROUPS | |
|---|---|---|---|---|---|---|
| | Overall Mean | Jan. | April | June | | Overall Mean |
| Volunteers | 3.72 | 3.84 | 3.57 | 3.80 | All Comparison Groups Combined | 3.59 |
| Precinct 6 | 4.00 | | | | | |
| Precinct 34 | 3.94 | | | | | |
| Precinct 24 | 4.00 | | | | | |

Furthermore, Operation Neighborhood groups tended to find their work more interesting than most jobs. As shown on Table 81, more of the volunteers and patrolmen in Precincts 34 and 24 felt this way than did the comparisons and patrolmen in Precinct 114 combined.

## TABLE 81: PATROLMAN'S OPINION OF HIS JOB
### (Adjusted for the Log of the Patrolman's Seniority)

Choose one of the following sets of characteristics which gives your
**individual impressions** of your job **during the last month**.

1. Boring  2. As interesting  3. More interesting  4. Very  5. Extremely
     as most jobs  than most jobs  interesting  interesting

| OPERATION NEIGHBORHOOD | | COMPARISON GROUPS | |
|---|---|---|---|
| | Overall Mean | | Overall Mean |
| Volunteers | 3.65 | Precinct 79 | 3.60 |
| Precinct 6 | 2.86 | Comparisons and Precinct 114 | 3.37 |
| Precinct 34 | 3.70 | | |
| Precinct 24 | 3.59 | | |

On this question, the log of the patrolmen's seniority was significant
at the .025 level. Men with more seniority were more likely to report that
their job was not interesting than were men with less seniority.

A patrolman's estimate of his usefulness to the public, as indicated
earlier, is a second measure of his interest. All Operation Neighborhood
groups, except Precinct 6, have scores which exceed that shown for the comparisons and Precinct 114. (See Table 82.)

## TABLE 82: PATROLMAN'S ESTIMATE OF POLICE USEFULNESS TO THE PUBLIC
### (Adjusted for Seniority of Three Years or Less)

1. Useless to  2. Not too use-  3. Somewhat  4. Very useful  5. Extremely
  the public    ful to the    useful to    to the    useful to
       public  the public  public  the public

| OPERATION NEIGHBORHOOD | | COMPARISON GROUPS | |
|---|---|---|---|
| | Overall Mean | | Overall Mean |
| Volunteers | 4.11 | Precinct 79 | 4.12 |
| Precinct 6 | 3.73 | Comparisons and Precinct 114 | 3.77 |
| Precinct 34 | 3.98 | | |
| Precinct 24 | 4.09 | | |

Another measure of job satisfaction was based on two questions in the patrol survey, specifically Questions 51 and 52. These questions referred the patrolmen to earlier questions which contained lists of activities and types of calls often encountered in police work. First, the patrolmen were asked to indicate those items most important to police work. Then, they were asked to indicate those activities or types of calls which they considered not very important to police work. The selections for each question were totaled (up to ten items were allowed) and then the value for Question 52 was subtracted from the value for Question 51. The figures shown in Table 83 represent the difference between the number of "important" and "unimportant" activities or types of calls. Significantly, an Operation Neighborhood group, the volunteers, has the highest score. In addition, there is an interesting trend in Precinct 34, where patrolmen selected more items as "important" in each successive wave of the survey.

TABLE 83:  INDEX OF JOB SATISFACTION BASED ON
SELECTION OF "IMPORTANT" AND "UNIMPORTANT" TASKS

(Adjusted for Seniority of Three Years or Less)

| OPERATION NEIGHBORHOOD | | | | | COMPARISON GROUPS | |
| --- | --- | --- | --- | --- | --- | --- |
| | Overall Mean | Jan. | April | June | | Overall Mean |
| Volunteers | 4.72 | | | | Precinct 79 | 4.12 |
| Precinct 6 | 4.65 | | | | Comparisons and Precinct 114 | 3.72 |
| Precinct 34 | 3.68 | 2.75 | 4.21 | 4.57 | | |
| Precinct 24 | 3.38 | | | | | |

The relationship between job satisfaction and performance is an important one. According to the data, more patrolmen in Precincts 6 and 34 believed that their jobs were frustrating than did the comparisons and Precinct 79 combined. In June, more patrolmen in Precinct 34, the volunteer group, and in comparison Precinct 114 reported that their jobs were frustrating than did the comparisons. Precinct 79 patrolmen indicated a higher level of frustration in June than they did in April.

Caution should be used in interpreting the figures shown in Table 84. The low figures for Operation Neighborhood groups may be due to a number of factors. On the one hand, they may reflect operational changes which cause frustration. On the other hand, they may be related to a higher level of expectation among team policemen. The goals of the Operation Neighborhood program were high. A patrolman's sincere desire to fulfill those goals could only be frustrated by the department's occasional failure to backup its commitment.

TABLE 84:  PATROLMAN'S SENSE OF FRUSTRATION OR ACCOMPLISHMENT

Choose one of the following sets of characteristics which gives your individual impressions of your job during the last month:

| 1. Extremely frustrating | 2. Frustrating | 3. About as frustrating as most jobs | 4. Gives some sense of accomplishment | 5. Gives great sense of accomplishment |
|---|---|---|---|---|

| OPERATION NEIGHBORHOOD | | COMPARISON GROUPS | |
|---|---|---|---|
|  | Overall Mean |  | Overall Mean |
| Volunteers | 2.92 | Precinct 114 | 2.83 |
| Precinct 6 | 2.38 | Comparisons and Precinct 79 | 3.15 |
| Precinct 34 | 2.72 |  |  |
| Precinct 24 | 2.93 |  |  |

It was believed that a patrolman's sense of accomplishment would be strengthened by the development of tactics that were more effective against crime. In order to test this belief, patrolmen were asked to estimate the effectiveness of a concentrated attack on the use of narcotics in their precinct. As shown in Table 85, the comparisons and patrolmen in Precincts 24 and 34 estimate the quickest successes. In interpreting these results, any supposed influence of the Operation Neighborhood program must, of course, be balanced by the individual characteristics of the neighborhoods involved.

TABLE 85: PATROLMAN'S ESTIMATE OF TIME REQUIRED TO
WIPE OUT USE OF NARCOTICS

(Adjusted for Seniority)

If your precinct spent all its time making narcotics cases, how long do
you believe it would take before narcotics use in the precinct became rare?

| OPERATION NEIGHBORHOOD | | COMPARISON GROUPS | |
|---|---|---|---|
| | Mean (In Months) | | Mean (In Months) |
| Volunteers | 84.7 | Comparisons | 61.5 |
| Precinct 6 | 104.0 | Precinct 114 | 86.6 |
| Precinct 34 | 65.6 | Precinct 79 | 101.6 |
| Precinct 24 | 68.7 | | |

On one additional question concerning how interesting the job is compared to a year ago, there were no important differences between Operation
Neighborhood groups and the comparison groups.

XII

DISPATCH OF NEIGHBORHOOD TEAMS

Operation Neighborhood guidelines state that, except for emergencies, team patrolmen should normally be assigned to work only in their team areas. Adherence to this stipulation was clearly fundamental to the proper implementation of the program.  Nevertheless, data from selected periods reveal a substantially different pattern of assignment.

The months selected for analysis were October 1971, December 1971, May 1972 and June 1972.  The information on radio runs was studied from two points of view.  First, radio runs within team areas were considered.  Those handled by team units were separated from those handled by non-team units. Second, the actual assignments of team units were broken into two categories-- runs inside team areas and runs outside team areas.  The results which are shown on Tables 86 and 87 are startling.  Approximately 50 percent of the radio runs within team areas were handled by non-team units.  Furthermore, approximately 52 percent of the runs by team units were out of their areas.

TABLE 86:  RADIO RUNS IN NEIGHBORHOOD TEAM AREAS
OCTOBER 1971, DECEMBER 1971, MAY 1972 AND JUNE 1972

| Type of Run | October Number | % | December Number | % | May Number | % | June* Number | % |
|---|---|---|---|---|---|---|---|---|
| Handled by NPT | 14,148 | 50.6 | 14,643 | 49.3 | 12,228 | 49.2 | 7,059 | 49.2 |
| Handled by non-NPT car | 13,816 | 49.4 | 15,040 | 50.7 | 12,709 | 50.8 | 7,287 | 50.8 |
| TOTAL | 27,964 | 100.0 | 29,683 | 100.0 | 24,937 | 100.0 | 14,346 | 100.0 |

*During June 13-30, 1972, a test of new priority call guidelines was made.

While these figures may seem rather clear cut, a number of important factors must be kept in mind. For example, these figures do not make allowances for instances when additional non-team sectors were assigned by precinct shift commanders to neighborhood police team units.[20] On such occasions, the dispatcher could send a team car out of its area because it was not designated solely as a team unit. In addition, the May and June figures do not include data for teams in Precincts 17, 24 and 77. These teams were cited as important sources of overlapping assignments in a May 1972 analysis of out-of-area runs.[21] Even with these reservations, the data show that there was no significant improvement in adhering to the above-mentioned guideline.

TABLE 87: RADIO RUNS BY NEIGHBORHOOD POLICE TEAMS
OCTOBER 1971, DECEMBER 1971, MAY 1972 AND JUNE 1972

| Location | October | | December | | May | | June* | |
|---|---|---|---|---|---|---|---|---|
| | Number | % | Number | % | Number | % | Number | % |
| In team areas | 14,148 | 50.4 | 14,643 | 47.7 | 12,228 | 47.7 | 7,059 | 48.1 |
| Out of team | 13,906 | 49.6 | 16,064 | 52.3 | 13,418 | 52.3 | 7,623 | 51.9 |
| TOTAL | 28,054 | 100.0 | 30,707 | 100.0 | 25,646 | 100.0 | 14,682 | 100.0 |

*During June 13-30, 1972, a test of new priority call guidelines was made.

---

20. An analysis of out-of-area assignments by Captain William Fox of the Communications Division for April 20, 1972 revealed that, on that date, 11.3 percent of the out-of-area runs were due to additional sector coverage.

21. This study for May 30, 1972 was also conducted by Captain William Fox. After correcting for additional sector coverage, multiple recording of the same call and the problem precincts (17, 24, and 77), it was found that, on average, 5.4 radio runs per team area (or about 2.7 hours per day) were made by teams out of their areas.

It was hoped that a change in dispatch procedures could be brought about by changing the definition of an "emergency call."[22] Consequently, on June 13, 1972, the Communications Division was directed to use the existing definition of "priority call" as the basis for deciding whether to dispatch team cars out of their assigned neighborhoods. The June data do not show any significant change in out-of-area runs as a result of the new guidelines. It is possible, however, the increasing manpower shortages in the department had an effect on the figures. A decline in out-of-area runs could have been masked by a corresponding increase in the practice of assigning team units to cover non-team sectors.

Obviously, the problem deserves further study. Present computer records might be changed to account for additional sector assignments. In addition, the patrol division should consider issuing guidelines to restrict the occasions on which additional sectors may be assigned to team units.

Although the data presented here do not show improvement in dispatch patterns, they do indicate that the volunteers and patrolmen in Precinct 34 were more satisfied with their dispatches than were the comparisons. (See Table 88.) These responses may reflect a difference in expectations. However, they may also be influenced by changes effected in the dispatch section near the end of June. The June averages were derived from data for the entire month; no special allowance was made for the June 13-30 period.

---

22. Such a recommendation was made in the Preliminary Evaluation of Operation Neighborhood, by Peter Bloch, March 1972 (The Urban Institute).

INDEX OF RADIO CAR DISPATCH

A weighted index of radio car dispatch was prepared from responses to three patrol survey questions. Those questions concerned the following:

- Dispatch from one end of the precinct to the other.[23]

- Dispatch to locations in the same sector.

- Dispatch to locations beyond the adjoining sector.

As shown in Table 88, an Operation Neighborhood group has the highest score. The information supplied by the men in the 34th Precinct appears to indicate that they were assigned more runs involving relatively short distances than any of the other groups. Between January and June, another Operation Neighborhood group--the volunteers--showed a marked improvement on this index. It was also found that men with more seniority tended to score higher, that is, to report more short runs, than did men with less seniority.

TABLE 88:  INDEX OF RADIO CAR DISPATCH

(Adjusted for Seniority of Patrolman)

| OPERATION NEIGHBORHOOD | | | | | COMPARISON GROUPS | |
|---|---|---|---|---|---|---|
| | Overall Mean | Jan. | April | June | | Overall Mean |
| Volunteers | 92.4 | 95.6 | 88.4 | 94.5 | All Comparison Groups Combined | 90.8 |
| Precinct 6 | 90.5 | | | | | |
| Precinct 34 | 98.7 | | | | | |
| Precinct 24 | 92.2 | | | | | |

Note:  Higher numbers equal shorter distances between runs.

---

23.  As part of the index's preparation, the answer to this question was subtracted.

DISPATCH EXPERIENCES

Across-Precinct Runs. When questioned about runs from one end of a
precinct to another, Precinct 34 patrolmen reported that 11.4 percent of
their runs were of that type. (See Table 89.)   This figure is not only
considerably lower than that for all the comparison groups combined (26.6
percent), but also considerably lower than that for any of the other team
groups.

Men with four or more years on the force, both in the total sample
population (all waves) and the June wave alone, reported a higher percentage
of long runs.   It is difficult to determine whether these figures are
accurate estimates of the patrolmen's runs or whether they are somewhat
inflated.   A patrolman's feeling that a long run is an imposition may cause
him to overestimate the percent of such runs actually assigned.

TABLE 89:   PERCENT OF RUNS ACROSS THE PRECINCT
(Adjusted for Seniority of Three Years or Less)

| OPERATION NEIGHBORHOOD | | COMPARISON GROUPS | |
|---|---|---|---|
| | Overall Mean | | Overall Mean |
| Volunteers | 25.2 | All Comparison Groups Combined | 26.6 |
| Precinct 6 | 20.7 | | |
| Precinct 34 | 11.4 | | |
| Precinct 24 | 23.2 | | |

Runs Beyond Adjoining Sector. On another question concerning dispatch
experiences, the Precinct 34 score stands out.   The men of this precinct
reported that only about 35.7 percent of their runs require them to go further
than the adjoining sector.   (See Table 90.)   Seniority, once again, is a
significant factor.   Men with less seniority reported a higher percentage of
runs beyond the adjoining sector than did men with more seniority.

TABLE 90: PERCENT OF RUNS BEYOND ADJOINING SECTOR

(Adjusted for the Log of Seniority of the Patrolman)

About what percent of your assigned radio runs require you to go further than the adjoining sector?

| OPERATION NEIGHBORHOOD | | COMPARISON GROUPS | |
|---|---|---|---|
| | Overall Mean | | Overall Mean |
| Volunteers | 41.5 | Precinct 114 | 43.7 |
| Precinct 6 | 51.7 | Comparisons and Precinct 79 | 50.0 |
| Precinct 34 | 35.7 | | |
| Precinct 24 | 49.8 | | |

Same Sector Runs. Patrolmen were asked to estimate what percent of their runs were located within the sector that they were patrolling at the time of the call. In the June wave, three of the four team groups reported a higher percentage of such calls than did all comparison groups combined. (See Table 91.)

TABLE 91: PERCENT OF RUNS IN SAME SECTOR

(Adjusted for Seniority of the Patrolman)

About what percent of your radio runs were in the same sector in which you were located when you got the call?

| OPERATION NEIGHBORHOOD | | | | | COMPARISON GROUPS | | | | |
|---|---|---|---|---|---|---|---|---|---|
| | Overall Mean | Jan. | April | June | | Overall Mean | Jan. | April | June |
| Volunteers | 35.4% | 43.1% | 27.6% | 38.1% | All Comparison Groups Combined | 29.1% | 35.5% | 31.3% | 21.5% |
| Precinct 6 | 18.5 | | | | | | | | |
| Precinct 34 | 34.4 | 34.9 | 30.2 | 38.5 | | | | | |
| Precinct 24 | 35.1 | | | | | | | | |

Between April and June, the volunteers and Precinct 34 patrolmen experienced an increase of "same sector" runs. This change was contrary to a department-wide trend. Between January and June, the groups in the sample generally reported a decrease in the percent of such runs.

Runs in Assigned Sector. Precinct 34 patrolmen reported a higher percentage of radio runs (55.1 percent) in the sector to which they were assigned than did any other group. (See Table 92.) On the other hand, the men in Precinct 6 reported the lowest percent of "in-sector" runs (27.1 percent.)[24]

On this question, men with more seniority tended to report a higher percentage of "in-sector" runs than did men with less seniority.

TABLE 92: PERCENT OF RUNS IN ASSIGNED SECTOR
(Adjusted for Seniority of the Patrolmen)

About what percent of your radio runs were in the sector to which you were assigned?

| OPERATION NEIGHBORHOOD | | COMPARISON GROUPS | |
|---|---|---|---|
| | Overall Mean | | Overall Mean |
| Volunteers | 45.0% | All Comparison Groups Combined | 43.6% |
| Precinct 6 | 27.1 | | |
| Precinct 34 | 55.1 | | |
| Precinct 24 | 42.1 | | |

The differences over time are not statistically significant. Nevertheless, the data do indicate that, relative to the rest of the department, the proportion of "in-sector" runs seems to be increasing in Precinct 34 and decreasing in Precinct 114.

When questioned about the fairness of dispatchers in assigning calls, Precinct 34 patrolmen expressed the greatest confidence in the fairness of their dispatchers. (See Table 93.) In the June wave, for instance, Precinct 34 registered a higher score than did the comparisons. This fact would indicate that patrolmen in Precinct 34 felt that dispatches were assigned fairly and equally, more than did the men of the above-mentioned comparison group.

---

24. According to an analysis of dispatch tapes, in May the men in Precinct 6 had only 36.9 percent of their runs within the team area. This figure is much lower than the average for all teams -- 47.7 percent.

TABLE 93:  PATROLMAN'S OPINION OF DISPATCH EQUALITY AND FAIRNESS
(Adjusted for Seniority of the Patrolman)

How often do radio dispatchers distribute calls fairly and equally?
1. Sometimes  2. Usually  3. Often  4. Almost always  5. Always

| OPERATION NEIGHBORHOOD | | COMPARISON GROUPS | |
|---|---|---|---|
| | Overall Mean | | Overall Mean |
| Volunteers | 2.69 | Comparisons | 2.78 |
| Precinct 6 | 3.09 | Precinct 114 | 2.87 |
| Precinct 34 | 3.65 | Precinct 79 | 2.89 |
| Precinct 24 | 2.73 | | |

It is not at all surprising that the overall score for Precinct 34 is higher than that for any other Operation Neighborhood or comparison group. As shown in Tables 89-92, the dispatch experiences of the men in this precinct were almost always more favorable than the experiences of the other groups.

It is interesting to note that men with more seniority seemed to feel that everyone was treated fairly more often than did men with less seniority.

DISPATCHES TO MEN ON FOOT OR SCOOTER PATROL

Patrolmen who were on foot or scooter patrol at least once in the week prior to completing the survey were asked about their dispatch experiences. Such men in comparison Precinct 79 reported receiving assignments from radio dispatchers while on foot or scooter patrol more often than all other groups (except Precinct 6) combined.

XIII

CONCLUDING OBSERVATIONS

In this report, certain aspects of the Operation Neighborhood program have received close attention; others have hardly been mentioned at all. This final chapter provides brief statements on a number of additional topics.

WAVE OF INNOVATION

As has been demonstrated, many innovative activities can be encompassed within a team policing program. Two that have been particularly successful for Operation Neighborhood are the use of civilian auxiliaries and the use of certain public relations techniques. Team commander reports indicate that, in some areas, unpaid volunteers are actively recruited by means of intensive campaigns and then utilized as translators in patrol cars, as foot beat patrolmen in areas where regular officers are not available, and as clerical assistants. Public relations for team members involves activities inside as well as outside of the department. For instance, the accomplishments of patrolmen who are team members, and some neighborhood teams as a whole, have been highlighted in a department newsletter. Furthermore, some team commanders have appeared on television (including cable television) and have developed a continuing coverage of team activities among small-circulation newspapers. These types of activities are highly visible and may tend to create the impression that more innovation is occurring under the Operation Neighborhood program than elsewhere. However, no quantitative measures have yet been accurately developed to test such an assumption.

OPERATION NEIGHBORHOOD TRAINING PROGRAM

A training program for neighborhood team commanders and patrolmen was established under the direction of Mr. George Gorman, who served as director. Two separate and distinct phases of the program were carried out. The first phase was conducted during the weeks of July 31 and August 14, 1972. It was effective in opening up lines of communication and developing a feeling of rapport between the team commanders and the trainers. All team commanders and ten trainers (five civilian, five police) participated. The second phase of the training program, which commenced in September 1972, emphasized field training. This phase concentrated on the five all Operation Neighborhood precincts (24th, 34th, 50th, 77th and 110th) and their 28 team commanders. Two trainers, one civilian and one police, were assigned to each precinct.

While the program has experienced a certain degree of success, it has failed to optimize its effect on team members and other department personnel. At least three limiting factors can be identified:

1. Tardiness of the training program (commencing well after the program was underway)

2. Problems of access

3. Failure of the department to tap an important source of information about the Operation Neighborhood program.

The reader will note from the dates given above that the training program commenced <u>over 18 months after Operation Neighborhood began in New York City.</u> Obviously, a great deal more might have been accomplished if the training program had begun sooner.

In the second phase, some of the trainers had difficulty gaining access to the teams they were supposed to train. In fact, in one precinct, it was necessary for the chief of patrol's office to intervene. The precinct commander finally did allow access to one of the five teams in the precinct, but it was the only one contacted by the trainers. Considering that only

five precincts were selected for this important training experience, it is

striking that the department did not insist that the trainers have access to

all of the teams.

The trainers involved in this endeavor remain an untapped source of

information about Operation Neighborhood. They are not only extremely

familiar with the program, but also willing and eager to talk about it. As

an "independent" group of professionals, their opinions should be of con-

siderable value to police officials (e.g., the commissioner, chief inspector

of patrol). The trainers have a stake in the success of Operation Neighbor-

hood, as a result, their suggestions should be heard.


## THE RELATIVE VALUE OF ACTIVITIES FROM
## THE PATROLMAN'S POINT OF VIEW

One of the major concerns of the Patrol Management Survey was measuring

the patrolman's attitude toward his job. It was hoped that certain questions

would provide information about the influence of Operation Neighborhood on

job satisfaction and on the patrolman's concept of the police function.

Judging by the results from Questions 51 and 52, Operation Neighborhood had

little or no success (1) in broadening the patrolman's concept of his job or

(2) in changing his opinion of the relative importance of police activities.

Before considering the results,[25] the reader needs to know more about

the form of the questions and the type of analysis involved. Briefly,

Questions 51 and 52 were concerned with judging the relative importance of

various police activities. They referred the officer completing the survey

to earlier questions (48, 49 and 50) which contained lists of activities and

---

25.  All data discussed here are from the June wave only.

types of calls often encountered in police work. Question 51 asked him to select activities or types of calls that he considered extremely important; and Question 52 asked him to select (from the same lists) the activities or calls that he considered not very important. In both cases, up to ten choices were allowed.

The answers to these questions were tabulated in order to compare the percentage of respondents who listed the various options as extremely important or not very important. Thus, the responses of the experimental and comparison groups can be measured against one another. As indicated by the figures on Table 94, the differences between the groups are not significant in most cases; therefore, only a few of the activities or types of calls will be discussed in detail.

Although 51 percent of all Operation Neighborhood groups and 56 percent of all comparison groups listed radio motor car patrol as extremely important, 68 percent of Precinct 24 and only 35 percent of Precinct 34 listed it as extremely important.

Plainclothes patrol was listed as extremely important by 45 percent of all Operation Neighborhood groups and by only 32 percent of all comparison groups (7 percent of the comparison groups listed it not very important). Twenty-one percent of Operation Neighborhood groups listed stakeouts as extremely important, but only 5 percent of the comparison groups did so. However, 35 percent of Precinct 34 and only 5 percent of Precinct 24 listed it as extremely important.

Forty-three percent of Operation Neighborhood groups as compared to 34 percent of comparison groups listed foot patrol as extremely important; 12 percent of all comparison groups listed it as not very important. While 61 percent of Precinct 24 listed foot patrol as extremely important, only 29 percent of Precinct 34 did so.

TABLE 94: PATROLMEN'S ESTIMATE OF THE IMPORTANCE OF VARIOUS
POLICE ACTIVITIES OR TYPES OF CALLS (IN PERCENT)

| TYPE OF ACTIVITY OR SERVICE CALL | ALL OPERATION NEIGHBORHOOD GROUPS | | ALL COMPARISON GROUPS | |
|---|---|---|---|---|
| | Extremely Important | Not Very Important | Extremely Important | Not Very Important |
| A. Radio Car Patrol | 51% | 0% | 56% | 5% |
| B. Investigating Specific Leads | 9 | 6 | 12 | 12 |
| C. Plainclothes Patrol | 45 | 0 | 32 | 7 |
| D. Stakeouts | 21 | 6 | 5 | 10 |
| E. Preliminary Investigation (at crime scene) | 11 | 6 | 10 | 2 |
| F. Foot Patrol | 43 | 6 | 34 | 12 |
| G. Family Dispute | 9 | 42 | 10 | 46 |
| H. Public Fight | 11 | 8 | 12 | 10 |
| J. Health Emergency | 38 | 13 | 17 | 37 |
| K. Abandoned Children | 28 | 4 | 24 | 7 |
| M. Crime in Progress | 79 | 0 | 73 | 0 |
| N. Policeman in Trouble | 87 | 4 | 80 | 0 |
| O. Looting of Several Stores | 43 | 4 | 17 | 5 |
| P. Observe Everything Carefully | 60 | 0 | 44 | 0 |
| R. Discuss Tactics With Your Partner | 11 | 8 | 24 | 0 |
| S. Observe Suspicious Locations With Care | 30 | 0 | 27 | 0 |
| T. Park Your Car and Talk to People | 19 | 21 | 20 | 39 |
| W. Check License Plates for Stolen Vehicles | 8 | 8 | 17 | 7 |
| X. Question Suspicious Individuals | 34 | 2 | 17 | 5 |
| Z. Break Up Groups of Loiterers | 6 | 21 | 12 | 7 |

Note: Certain letters of the alphabet were eliminated from the list to avoid reading errors.

Thirty-eight percent of all Operation Neighborhood groups listed health emergency as extremely important and 13 percent listed it not very important. In the comparison groups, on the other hand, 37 percent listed health emergency as not very important and only 17 percent listed it as extremely important.

A service call involving the looting of several stores was considered extremely important by 43 percent of all Operation Neighborhood groups, but by only 17 percent of all comparison groups.

A family dispute service call was considered not very important by 42 percent of all Operation Neighborhood groups and by 46 percent of all comparison groups. About 10 percent of both groups considered it extremely important. However, 59 percent of Precinct 34 listed family disputes as not very important and no one in Precinct 34 listed it as extremely important.

About 20 percent of both groups listed park, walk and talk as extremely important; however, 21 percent of Operation Neighborhood groups and 39 percent of the comparison groups listed it as not very important. In addition, only 5 percent of Precinct 24 and 11 percent of Precinct 6 listed park, walk and talk as extremely important, while 28 percent of Precinct 6 did so.[26]

Questioning suspicious individuals was listed as extremely important by 34 percent of the Operation Neighborhood groups compared to 17 percent of the comparison groups. On the other hand, 21 percent of Operation Neighborhood groups listed breaking up groups of loiterers as not very important, compared to 7 percent of all comparison groups.

---

26. In light of the emphasis on park, walk and talk in Operation Neighborhood and the department, this was an unexpected finding.

INDEX OF CHANGE

As the reader may remember, there were several questions in the patrol survey which asked the patrolman to compare job-related experiences at the time of the survey with such experiences a year earlier. These questions were not designed to measure similar things and combining them into an "index of change" is something of an afterthought. Nevertheless, the results could be of interest. For instance, if Operation Neighborhood teams were producing favorable change at a faster rate than the comparison groups, one might expect that this index would show some advantage to Operation Neighborhood groups. However, the data presented in Tables 95, 96 and 97 do not indicate any significant differences between the groups—either on the index or the individual questions.

TABLE 95: INDEX OF CHANGE

(Raw June Scores)

| OPERATION NEIGHBORHOOD | | COMPARISON GROUPS | |
|---|---|---|---|
| | June | | June |
| Volunteers | 100.3 | Comparisons | 99.1 |
| Precinct 6 | 100.6 | Precinct 114 | 98.8 |
| Precinct 34 | 100.7 | Precinct 79 | 98.8 |
| Precinct 24 | 100.2 | | |

Standard Deviation = 2.94

TABLE 96:  PATROLMAN'S ESTIMATE OF CITIZEN WILLINGNESS
TO SERVE AS A COMPLAINING WITNESS*

(Adjusted for Seniority of Less than Three Years)

When you investigated crimes and asked people to be complaining witnesses <u>during the last month</u>, was cooperation, <u>compared to a year ago,</u> getting:

1. Much worse   2. A little   3. About the   4. A little   5. Much
                    worse          same            better          better

| OPERATION NEIGHBORHOOD | | | | | COMPARISON GROUPS | |
|---|---|---|---|---|---|---|
| | Overall Mean | Jan. | April | June | | Overall Mean |
| Volunteers | 3.05 | 3.24 | 3.24 | 2.64 | All Comparison Groups Combined | 3.23 |
| Precinct 6 | 3.47 | | | | | |
| Precinct 34 | 3.71 | | | | | |
| Precinct 24 | 3.50 | | | | | |

*See Patrol Management Survey, Question 20.

TABLE 97:  PATROLMAN'S ESTIMATE OF CITIZEN WILLINGNESS
TO REPORT A BURGLARY*

(Adjusted for the Log of the Seniority of Patrolmen)

In your opinion, <u>during the last month</u>, how likely were people to report a residential burglary <u>compared to a year ago</u>:

1. Much more   2. A little      3. About the   4. A little      5. Much less
   likely          more likely      same            less likely      likely

| OPERATION NEIGHBORHOOD | | | | | COMPARISON GROUPS | | | | |
|---|---|---|---|---|---|---|---|---|---|
| | Overall Mean | Jan. | April | June | | Overall Mean | Jan. | April | June |
| Volunteers | 2.59 | 2.43 | 2.64 | 2.66 | Precinct 114 | 2.79 | 2.86 | 2.65 | 2.91 |
| Precinct 6 | 2.27 | | | 2.27 | Comparisons and Precinct 79 | 2.65 | 2.14 | 2.92 | 2.50 |
| Precinct 34 | 2.24 | 1.91 | 2.69 | 2.27 | | | | | |
| Precinct 24 | 2.78 | | | 2.78 | | | | | |

*See Patrol Management Survey, Question 21.

APPENDIXES

APPENDIX A

T.O.P. 364
Police Department, City of New York

APPENDIX B

Patrol Management Survey

APPENDIX C

Method of Constructing Indexes

*APPENDIX A*

*T.O.P. 364*

*POLICE DEPARTMENT*
*CITY OF NEW YORK*

*December 30, 1970*

*TO ALL COMMANDS:*

*Subject:   OPERATION NEIGHBORHOOD - NEIGHBORHOOD POLICE TEAM PROGRAM*

*1.    Effective 0001 hours, January 1, 1971, the initial Operation Neighborhood Project will be implemented in the 77th Precinct.*

*2.    Under the direction of the precinct commander, a volunteer Sergeant has been assigned to command the patrol personnel within a radio motor patrol sector.  A number of volunteer patrolmen have been selected for this project and will form a team which is responsible to the Neighborhood Police Team Commander.  The number of patrolmen selected is proportional to the workload. These patrolmen will normally work only in the sector territory.  The Neighborhood Police Team Commander and his men have the responsibility for providing patrol services within this sector on a twenty-four hour basis.*

*3.    The purpose of this program is to determine if greater efficiency can be produced by granting authority to the precinct commander to assign sergeants and patrolmen to a specific area of the precinct.  In addition, authority is granted to the Neighborhood Team to devise tactics for coping with the sector's crime and other police related problems.*

*4.    It is realized that in police work problems are numerous, a great many beyond our control, and it is also realized that many of today's operating procedures are just not producing the desired effect.  For many years our operating procedures have placed a main emphasis on the prevention of misconduct and many of the restrictive features of this emphasis have had a detrimental effect on police-public relations.  While misconduct will continue to be fought with every means possible, the main emphasis of our operating procedures will now be service to the public.  Let our actions be guided not by "There is nothing I can do," but by "How can I help?"*

*5.    Arrests will continue to be made.  Where voluntary compliance can not be obtained in cases of minor violations, summonses will continue to be served.  It is expected that by granting greater authority to assist the public, and by assigning specific personnel to an area with the authority to do a job, in time there will be an increase in cooperation and a reduction in apathy on the part of many of the people of the area.*

6. *The Department, by initiating this program, is indicating its belief in the ability of first-line supervisors and patrolmen to assume more responsibility and to demonstrate to the citizens of the City of New York that one of their greatest assets is the policemen who serve them. This program will also provide the precinct commander with subordinate personnel specifically responsible for areas of the precinct. The Desk Officer will have a definite source for referral of problems. The Sergeant's duties and authority will be expanded in keeping with his rank, and the Patrolmen will have the opportunity for more varied and interesting service.*

7. *Attached are operating instructions to be followed in connection with the Neighborhood Police Team Program. All provisions of the Rules and Procedures or other Department orders in conflict with these instructions are temporarily suspended in the area of the 77th Precinct where the Neighborhood Police Team Program is in operation.*

*BY DIRECTION OF THE POLICE COMMISSIONER.*

> *MICHAEL J. CODD*
> *Chief Inspector*

Distribution:

*TO ALL COMMANDS*

Inactive Date:

*Upon publication of subsequent orders.*

*POLICE DEPARTMENT*
*CITY OF NEW YORK*

*OPERATING INSTRUCTIONS*
*NEIGHBORHOOD POLICE TEAM PROGRAM*

I. *RESPONSIBILITIES OF THE NEIGHBORHOOD POLICE TEAM COMMANDER*

A. *The Team Commander will have discretionary judgment in supplying and utilizing patrol resources within the sector Territory. However, the relationship of the Team Commander to his superiors in the chain of command will remain the same. He will be subject to all the provisions of the Rules and Procedures except as otherwise provided for in the Operating Instructions.*

B. *The Team Commander will be free to determine his own working hours. However, the number of hours worked must average 40 hours per week. We will report his presence to the Desk Officer at the beginning and the conclusion of each period of duty and a blotter entry to this effect will be made. When reporting for duty he will inform the Desk Officer of his anticipated activities. If any special precinct duties are expected of him during his period of duty, the Desk Officer will inform him of their nature. By Friday of each week, the Team Commander will furnish the precinct commanding officer with his work schedule for the forthcoming week.*

C. *The Team Commander, whether or not he is on duty, is responsible for the activities of the Team patrolmen. Team patrolmen are responsible for reporting to the Team Commander all incidents in which they encounter difficulties. If the difficulty concerns conflicting orders or instructions from another superior officer, the Team Commander will confer with the other superior officer concerning the conflict. The precinct commanding officer will resolve any conflicts that cannot be resolved by the Team Commander and the other superior officer. The Team Commander is responsible for conferring with Sergeants and other superior officers who have observed the Team patrolmen in the performance of their duties, so that he can determine whether they are performing adequately when he is not on duty. He shall confer frequently with the precinct commanding officer regarding conditions in the sector and the performance of his Team.*

D. *After consultation with the precinct commanding officer, the Team Commander shall be responsible for the assignment of Team patrolmen to work during those hours which he believes are likely to control crime and to serve the community living within the sector territory. However, the Team Commander and his men have the responsibility for providing patrol services within the sector on a twenty-four hour basis. Team patrolmen may be required to work*

*T.O.P. 364*

*either in uniform or in civilian clothes. They may also be required to investigate crime, to meet with individuals designated by the Team Commander, and to perform other special duties as required by the Team Commander. In the case of any assignment of a Team patrolman to duty in civilian clothes, the precinct commander must be informed and his concurrence obtained. If the precinct commanding officer is not available and the Team Commander believes that such a civilian clothes assignment is necessary for the accomplishment of his mission, he will notify the Desk Officer of such assignment and a blotter entry to this effect shall be made. As soon as he is available, the precinct commanding officer shall be advised of the civilian clothes assignment. The Team Commander's monthly report shall include the number of periods of duty worked in civilian clothes by members of the Team and the reasons therefor.*

E. *Although the Team Commander is responsible for formulating the work hours and assignment of the patrolmen of the Team, in no case will any assignment to hours of duty not in accordance with an authorized Department duty chart be made unless the concurrence of the patrolman so assigned is obtained.*

F. *By Friday of each week, the Team Commander shall furnish to the precinct commanding officer the work assignments of the Team Patrolmen for the forthcoming week.*

G. *The Team Commander is responsible for establishing a procedure for informing the Team Patrolmen of orders and instructions concerning the operation of the sector. Records concerning crime, other conditions within the sector, and Team Activities shall be maintained and this information shall be disseminated to the members of the Team.*

H. *The Team Commander shall hold frequent group conferences with members of the Team. At these conferences, problems, conditions, or any other matters affecting the operation of the sector shall be discussed.*

I. *The Team Commander shall submit monthly reports by the 5th of the following month concerning the operation of the sector. These original reports shall be forwarded through channels to the Office of the Chief Inspector, Room 108. The report shall include:*

1. *A statement of his activities for the past month*

2. *A statement concerning the activity of the Team for the past month*

3. *Recommendations for improving the sector operation*

4. *Any other pertinent information*

5. *Problems encountered and measures taken to overcome them*

6. *Local Press and Community Newsletter articles concerning the Neighborhood Police Team shall be attached to the report.*

J. *The Team Commander and Team patrolmen are encouraged to assist the people of the sector territory, including the obtaining of assistance from other city agencies. Within guidelines established by the Team Commander, they are authorized to make direct contact with other city agencies for this purpose.*

K. *The Team Commander and Team patrolmen are encouraged to give to the public the widest possible verbal and written dissemination of information regarding the existence and purposes of this program. The Team Commander is authorized to prepare and distribute pertinent printed matter concerning police-community related operations. He is also authorized to secure the cooperation of local publications, as well as public and private agencies and organizations to further the goals of this program.*

L. *One of the purposes of this program is to get the people of the neighborhood to know the members of the force assigned to it. The Team Commander is authorized to prepare and distribute literature with pertinent information informing the public whom to contact for assistance and who was assigned to their individual complaints.*

M. *The Team Commander shall initiate a system of visits to civic and community organizations so that he or other members of the Team would be available to explain the Neighborhood Police Team Program and to discuss other related matters.*

II. *RESPONSIBILITIES OF NEIGHBORHOOD POLICE TEAM PATROLMEN*

A. *Team patrolmen are responsible for performing the duties assigned to them by the Team Commander and other superior officers of the Department. When the Team Commander is not present, Team patrolmen are subject to supervision by the other superior officers of the precinct. If in the absence of the Team Commander, any order or instruction is given to a patrolman by another superior officer that is in conflict with an order or instruction previously given by the Team Commander, the patrolman shall inform the superior officer of the conflict and be guided by his decision. Upon the return of the Team Commander, the patrolman will inform him of the conflict.*

B. *When not on assignment, members of the Team assigned to radio motor patrol duty have the authority to secure and leave the RMP car and patrol on foot within the sector. In addition to checking on possible crime locations such as hallways, roofs, yards and other similar locations, Team patrolmen are encouraged to speak with and make known their presence to residents, business people and other* members of the community within their sector. However, while on this type of patrol, Team patrolmen shall maintain constant radio contact by means of walkie-talkies and shall be responsible for responding to radio runs. The provisions of this paragraph also apply to members of the Team performing scooter or foot patrol duty.

C. If in the opinion of a member of the Team, the rendering of assistance to people in the sector area can be accomplished by transporting a civilian in an RMP car, authority is granted for him to do so. In any instance where this is done, the radio dispatcher will be notified at the beginning and conclusion of the trip, and details entered on the Daily Activity Report. These trips will be limited to those which tend to reflect credit on the Department, such as transporting sick and injured to a hospital, if practical when no ambulance available, and would not include those of personal benefit, such as payroll or bank escorts.

D. In order to render assistance to the public, members of the Team are authorized to push disabled autos with an RMP car if this service is necessary and practical. Other practical measures to assist disabled motorists are also authorized.

E. The Team Patrolmen have a responsibility to attend group conferences conducted by the Team Commander. They have a responsibility to make suggestions or criticisms for improving the operation of the Team.

F. Daily Activity Reports will be prepared by members of the Team and submitted to the Team Commander at the end of each tour.

III. GENERAL INSTRUCTIONS

A. RADIO RUN SERVICE. Team Patrolmen will normally be assigned to work only in the sector territory. As such, they have the responsibility for servicing all the radio runs occurring within the sector. If the sector RMP is unable to respond, the Communications Division dispatcher when possible will have the radio run serviced by other members of the Team performing patrol within the sector. Only if the radio run is of an emergency nature or requires instant response, will RMP crews from other sectors be dispatched into the Team territory. The same standard will apply for dispatching the Team RMP car out of the sector territory.

B. VACATION SELECTIONS. For the purpose of this program, the Team Commander and Team patrolmen will select their vacations separately from other members of the precinct. This is necessary to provide for continued patrol coverage of the sector by members of the Team. In addition, members of the Team will be permitted to select vacation periods of one week duration if they so desire.

C.  *COURT ATTENDANCE.  The provisions of Departmental orders concerning overtime and lost time shall apply to members of the Team.  However, members of the Team who effect arrests while performing duty on the 3rd or 4th platoons and who are required to attend court on the following day tour may at their option choose to attend court on an overtime basis providing they agree to perform duty on the following 3rd or 4th platoon if so scheduled.*

D.  *COOPERATION.  The cooperation of all precinct personnel is vital if this program is to succeed.  The Team Commander and members of his Team must be kept apprised of conditions affecting their sector. Messages and requests for assistance must be promptly brought to their attention.*

E.  *MISCONDUCT.  Members of this program are reminded that the Department is aware of the possibilties for misconduct in this program. The applicable provisions of the Rules and Procedures and the various laws pertaining to misconduct remain in full force and effect.*

APPENDIX   B

February 2, 1972

<u>ANONYMOUS</u>

PATROL MANAGEMENT SURVEY


The New York City Police Department has initiated many programs and desires to know how they affect the patrol force.  Please read this survey carefully and answer with your own opinions and to the best of your knowledge.  Your identity will never be known by anyone. Your <u>answer sheet</u> will be deposited by you, inside a plain brown envelope, in a pile of other answers.

When the question has several choices given as answers, please check the letter on the answer sheet for the answer with which you most closely agree.  If there is a blank, please put in a <u>single</u> number (from 0 to 9999), however difficult that may be.  The number may be a rough guess, but a <u>single</u> number is needed in order to score this survey.

Thank you for assisting your Police Department in helping to evaluate its programs and improve your job.


NOTE:  <u>If you have been a member of the police force for less than one year</u>, then you will have difficulty answering questions which ask you to compare what has happened in the last month to what happened a year ago.  Since you were not on the police force that long, please answer that type of question by comparing what happened in the <u>last month</u> to what happened in the <u>first month in which you were on active duty</u>.

December 21, 1971

PATROL MANAGEMENT SURVEY

The New York City Police Department has initiated many programs and desires to know how they affect the patrol force. Please read this survey carefully and answer with your own opinions and to the best of your knowledge. Your identity will never be known by anyone. Your answer sheet will be deposited by you, inside a plain brown envelope, in a pile of other answers.

When the question has several choices given as answers, please check the letter on the answer sheet for the answer with which you most closely agree. If there is a blank, please put in a single number (from 0 to 9999), however difficult that may be. The number may be a rough guess, but a single number is needed in order to score this survey.

Thank you for assisting your Police Department in helping to evaluate its programs and improve your job.

NOTE: If you have been a member of the police force for less than one year, then you will have difficulty answering questions which ask you to compare what has happened in the last month to what happened a year ago. Since you were not on the police force that long, please answer that type of question by comparing what happened in the last month to what happened in the first month in which you were on active duty.

1.  How cooperative has the public been lately when you needed information about a crime?

    A. Almost never    B. Seldom    C. Sometimes    D. Usually    E. Almost always
       help               help          help            help          help

2.  How often does a witness of a crime agree to appear in court as a complaining witness?

    A. Almost never    B. Seldom    C. Sometimes    D. Usually    E. Almost always

FOR THE FOLLOWING QUESTIONS PUT IN THE BLANK ON YOUR ANSWER SHEET HOW MANY TIMES THE EVENT OCCURRED. WRITE A ZERO ("0") IF THAT IS APPROPRIATE. PLEASE PUT ONE NUMBER (FROM 0 to 9999) IN EVERY BLANK.

3.  About how many times have people insulted or verbally abused you in the last month?

4.  About how many times have people threatened or attempted to injure you in the last month?

5.  About how many times have citizens complimented you in the last month?

6.  About how many civilians other than informants do you talk to on a regular basis in the course of your duties?

7.  In your opinion, about what percent of people who had a $40 item stolen from their car would report the incident to the police?

8.  What percentage of bystanders do you think would like you to be physically harmed when you make an arrest on the street after dark in your precinct?

9.  What percent of the people in your precinct belong to groups which regularly oppose police?

10. What percent of the people in your precinct belong to groups which support the police politically or as volunteers?

11. In the last month, about what percent of businessmen in the precinct would have liked to give a policeman a meal or small tip because they want him to be friendly and to be sympathetic if they should have a problem in the future.

12. In the last month, about how many people indicated (although you could not prove it) that they might like to do you a favor if you would give them at least some minor special consideration?

13. Including informants and all others, how many people have given you information about criminals or criminal activities in the last month?

14. How many informants have given you information about criminals or criminal activities in the last month?

15. How many people <u>other than informants</u> whom you talk to on a regular basis have given you information about criminals or criminal activities <u>in the last month?</u>

16. If your precinct spent all its time making narcotics cases, how long do you believe it would take before narcotics use in the precinct became rare?

17. How often do people <u>help</u> by calling for assistance when they see that a policeman is in trouble?

    A. Almost     B. Seldom     C. Sometimes     D. Often     E. Almost
       never                                                 always

18. How often will people volunteer or agree to testify in a policeman's behalf if they know that he has been unjustifibly accused of misconduct?

    A. Almost never    B. Seldom    C. Sometimes    D. Often    E. Almost Always

19. When you have responded to a public argument or street fight <u>during the last month</u>, was bystander hostility <u>compared to a year ago</u>, getting

    A. Much     B. A little     C. About the     D. A little     E. Much
       worse        worse        same           better         better

20. When you investigated crimes and asked people to be complaining witnesses <u>during the last month</u>, was cooperation, <u>compared to a year ago</u>, getting

    A. Much     B. A little     C. About the    D. A little     E. Much
       worse        worse        same        better        better

21. In your opinion, <u>during the last month</u>, how likely were people to report a residential burglary to police <u>compared to a year ago</u>:

    A. Much more     B. A little     C. About the     D. A little    E. Much less
       likely        more likely     same        less likely   likely

22. How satisfied are you with your pay?

    A. Completely    B. Generally     C. Not too        D. Dissatisfied    E. Very
       satisfied      satisfied       satisfied                          dissatisfied

23. How often <u>in the last month</u> have your job activities given you satisfaction?

    A. Almost     B. Seldom     C. Sometimes     D. Often     E. Almost always
       never

24. When you respond to a situation, how much of what you do is the result of your own judgment or discretion (as opposed to "just following orders" or doing what the law requires)?

    A. Almost no     B. Some discretion    C. Often use     D. Almost     E. Always
       discretion or    or judgment       discretion      always use    use
       judgment used                    or judgment    discretion    discre-
                                              or judgment   tion or
                                                                      judgment

25. How satisfied are you with your work schedule?

    A. Very    B. Somewhat    C. Mildly    D. Somewhat    E. Very
                                              dissatisfied    dissatisfied

26. <u>In the last month</u>, how satisfied were you with your work schedule <u>compared to a year ago</u>?

    A. Much less    B. A little    C. About the    D. A little    E. Much more
       satisified       less        same       more       satisfied
                satisfied                     satisfied

CHOOSE ONE OF THE FOLLOWING SETS OF CHARACTERISTICS WHICH GIVES YOUR <u>INDIVIDUAL IMPRESSIONS</u> OF YOUR JOB <u>DURING THE LAST MONTH</u> AND CHECK THE APPROPRIATE LETTER ON YOUR ANSWER SHEET:

27. A. Boring    B. As interesting    C. More interesting    D. Very    E. Extremely
               as most jobs      than most jobs     interesting     interesting

28. A. Extremely    B. Frustrating    C. About as    D. Gives some    E. Gives
       frustrating                  frustrating     sense of       great
                              as most jobs   accomplish-   sense of
                                           ment       accomplishment

29. A. A little    B. Quite    C. Pretty    D. Very    E. Extremely
       risky       risky      dangerous    dangerous    dangerous

30. A. Useless    B. Not too    C. Somewhat    D. Very useful    E. Extremely
       to the       useful to    useful to     to the public   useful to
       public      the public   the public                 the public

31. A. Looked down    B. Not appreciated    C. Mildly    D. Appreciated    E. Greatly
       on by the      by the public     appreciated   by the     appreciated
       public                       by the public  public     by the
                                                      public

32. How many patrolmen did you see socially during the last month when you were off duty?

33. Is there one sergeant assigned to your precinct to whom you **regularly talk about** your job and your job **problems**?

    A. Yes                B. No

34. <u>In the last month</u>, how satisfied were you <u>compared to a year ago</u> with your opportunity to do interesting and rewarding work?

    A. Much less    B. A little less    C. About the    D. A little more    E. Much more
       satisfied       satisfied       same        satisfied      satisfied

35. About what percent of your precinct's policemen are highly motivated in their job and do even more than is **required**?

36. What is your reaction to the principle that, "A good leader should be strict with people under him in order to improve their performance."?

    A. Strongly    B. Mildly    C. Not     D. Mildly      E. Strongly
       agree         agree       sure       disagree        disagree

37. How often do radio dispatchers distribute calls fairly and equally?

    A. Sometimes      B. Usually     C. Often     D. Almost always      E. Always

38. How much do your superiors know about how well you do your job?

    A. No one person    B. They have some    C. They know    D. They are well
       knows enough        knowledge about     generally       informed about
       to judge my         how I do my job     how well        most things
       work fairly                          I do my job     I do on the job

    E. They are well
       informed about
       everything I do on
       the job

39. When you have complaints about your job, how understanding or sympathetic are your superiors?

    A. Very           B. Fair but not   C. Somewhat    D. Reasonably   E. Very
       unsympathetic     sympathetic      sympathetic      sympathetic     sympathetic

40. How often in the last month have you suggested to your superiors the use of new or better methods or tactics?

41. In the last month, how many of your suggestions of new or better methods or tactics were accepted or used by your superiors?

42. How effective have precinct police been in the last month in making arrests supported by sufficient admissable evidence to lead to a conviction?

    A. Very        B. Somewhat    C. Reasonably   D. Very        E. Extremely
       ineffective      effective       effective       effective       effective

43. How effective have precinct police been in the last month in harassing criminals by arresting them on charges that probably will not lead to convictions?

    A. Very        B. Somewhat    C. Reasonably   D. Very        E. Extremely
       ineffective      effective       effective       effective       effective

    F. Not applicable (such
       arrests are not attempted)

44. In the last month, how effective have precinct police been in preventing crime by preventive patrol?

    A. Very        B. Somewhat    C. Reasonably   D. Very        E. Extremely
       ineffective      effective       effective       effective       effective

45. __In the last month,__ how effective have precinct police been in __preventing__ crime by __aggressive patrol practices__ such as stop and frisk?

   A. Very        B. Somewhat   C. Reasonably D. Very       E. __Extremely__
      ineffective    effective      effective     effective     effective

   F. Not applicable
      (The precinct does
      not use these techniques.)

46. __In the last month,__ how often have you practiced __aggressive patrol practices__ such as stop and frisk?

   A. Almost   B. Seldom   C. Sometimes   D. Often   E. Very often
      never

47. __In the last month,__ how often have you been following up specific leads or information about a crime or criminals __compared to last year?__

   A. Much   B. Less   C. About the   D. More   E. Much   F. Not applicable (I have
      less              same                     more       never done this.)

48. Please list the following activities on your answer sheet. Put the __letter__ of the __most important__ activity (that is, the activity which you feel is most likely to be important __to the public__) at the __top__ and the letter of the least important at the bottom. As nearly as possible, please try to make the list one of decreasing importance so that whenever an activity is __below__ another it is __less__ important to the public.

   Please put one letter in every blank on the answer sheet.

   A. Radio Car Patrol
   B. Investigating Specific Leads
   C. Plainclothes Patrol
   D. Stakeouts
   E. Preliminary Investigation (at crime scene)
   F. Foot Patrol

49. Please list the following kinds of calls on your answer sheet. Put the __letter__ of the __most important__ call (that is, the call in which you feel you are most likely to perform an __important public service__) at the __top__ and the letter of the least important at the bottom. As nearly as possible, please try to make the list one of decreasing importance so that calls calling for __less important public service__ always will be __below__ those that are more important.

   Please put one letter in every blank on the answer sheet.

   G. Family Dispute
   H. Public Fight
   J. Health Emergency
   K. Abandoned Children
   M. Crime in Progress
   N. Policeman in Trouble
   O. Looting of Several Stores

50. When a police officer rides in a radio car he sometimes has periods in which no run has been assigned. When that happens, many useful things can be done. Please list the following activities from those which are most important to those that are least important. Put the most important at the top and, in order of decreasing importance, the least important at the bottom.

   Please put one letter in every blank on the answer sheet.
   P.  Observe Everything Carefully
   R.  Discuss Tactics With Your Partner
   S.  Observe Suspicious Locations With Care
   T.  Park Your Car and Talk to People
   W.  Check License Plates for Stolen Vehicles
   X.  Question Suspicious Individuals
   Z.  Break Up Groups of Loiterers

51. Looking back at the last three questions (48, 49, 50), you may think that some of the choices are extremely important to police work or are extremely important types of calls for a policeman to handle. On your answer sheet, please put the letter of at least one item you consider extremely important. You may list up to ten choices.

   FOR THIS QUESTION YOU DO NOT NEED TO FILL IN ALL THE BLANKS. LIST ONLY THE LETTERS FOR THE CHOICES YOU CONSIDER EXTREMELY IMPORTANT TO POLICE WORK.

52. Looking back again at questions 48, 49, 50, you may think that some of the choices are not very important to police work or are not very important types of calls for a policeman to handle. On your answer sheet, please put the letter of at least one item you consider not very important. You may list up to ten choices.

   FOR THIS QUESTION YOU DO NOT NEED TO FILL IN ALL THE BLANKS. LIST ONLY THE LETTERS FOR THE CHOICES YOU CONSIDER NOT VERY IMPORTANT TO POLICE WORK.

ANSWER THE NEXT FOUR QUESTIONS, 53-56, ONLY IF YOU WORKED IN A RADIO CAR AT LEAST ONCE LAST WEEK. PLEASE ANSWER THE REST OF THE QUESTIONS ANYWAY.

53. About what percent of your radio runs take you practically from one end of the precinct to the other?

54. About what percent of your assigned radio runs require you to go further than the adjoining sector?

55. About what percent of your radio runs was in the same sector in which you were then located when you got the call?

56. About what percent of your radio runs was in the sector to which you were assigned?

ANSWER THE NEXT QUESTION ONLY IF YOU EITHER WORKED ON FOOT PATROL OR ON A SCOOTER
AT LEAST ONCE LAST WEEK.  PLEASE ANSWER THE REST OF THE QUESTIONS ANYWAY.

57. When you worked on foot patrol or on a scooter, how often were you given
    assignments by the radio dispatcher?

    A. Never    B. Rarely    C. Sometimes    D. Often    E. Very Often

58. Do you think your job is getting better or worse? How? PLEASE ANSWER
    ON THE BACK OF ANSWER SHEET.

PLEASE ANSWER EACH OF THE FOLLOWING QUESTIONS BY PUTTING A CHECK IN ONE OR TWO
BLANKS ON YOUR ANSWER SHEET, DEPENDING ON WHICH CHOICES APPLY TO YOU.

59. Experiment with the number of sergeants (Span):

    A. In effect in my Precinct    B. Not in my Precinct

60. Operations Lieutenant:

    A. In effect in my Precinct    B. Not in my Precinct

61. Anti-Crime:

    A. In effect in my Precinct    B. I am part of the Program    C. Not in my Precinct

62. Community Relations Program:

    A. In effect in my Precinct    B. I am part of the Program    C. Not in my Precinct

63. Detective Specialization:

    A. In effect in my borough    B. Not in my borough

64. Neighborhood Police Team:

    A. In effect in my Precinct    B. I am part of the Program    C. Not in my Pretinct

65. Neighborhood Police Training:

    A. In effect in my Precinct    B. I am part of the Program    C. Not in my Precinct

66. Women in the Patrol Force:

    A. In effect in my Precinct    B. I am part of the Program    C. Not in my Precinct

67. About how many years have you been in the police department?

68. About how long have you been in your precinct?

69. Have you been on patrol, plainclothes duty or foot duty at least one week
    in the last month?  (Add up the time spent on all these activities.)

    A.  Yes         B.  No

70. How would you improve the patrol force? PLEASE ANSWER ON THE BACK OF
    ANSWER SHEET.

ANSWER SHEET
(Please return inside plain brown envelope.)

1. __ __ __ __ __
   A  B  C  D  E

2. __ __ __ __ __
   A  B  C  D  E

3. __ __ __ __

4. __ __ __ __

5. __ __ __ __

6. __ __ __ __

7. __ __ __ percent

8. __ __ __ percent

9. __ __ __ percent

10. __ __ __ percent

11. __ __ __ percent

12. __ __ __ __

13. __ __ __ __

14. __ __ __ __

15. __ __ __ __

16. __ __ __ years
    __ __ months

17. __ __ __ __ __
   A  B  C  D  E

18. __ __ __ __ __
   A  B  C  D  E

19. __ __ __ __ __
   A  B  C  D  E

20. __ __ __ __ __
   A  B  C  D  E

21. __ __ __ __ __
   A  B  C  D  E

22. __ __ __ __ __
   A  B  C  D  E

23. __ __ __ __ __
   A  B  C  D  E

24. __ __ __ __ __
   A  B  C  D  E

25. __ __ __ __ __
   A  B  C  D  E

26. __ __ __ __ __
   A  B  C  D  E

27. __ __ __ __ __
   A  B  C  D  E

28. __ __ __ __ __
   A  B  C  D  E

29. __ __ __ __ __
   A  B  C  D  E

30. __ __ __ __ __
   A  B  C  D  E

31. __ __ __ __ __
   A  B  C  D  E

32. __ __ __ __

33. __ __
   A (Yes)  B (No)

34. __ __ __ __ __
   A  B  C  D  E

35. __ __ __ percent

36. __ __ __ __ __
   A  B  C  D  E

37. __ __ __ __ __
   A  B  C  D  E

38. __ __ __ __ __
   A  B  C  D  E

39. __ __ __ __ __
   A  B  C  D  E

40. __ __ __ __

41. __ __ __

42. __ __ __ __ __
   A  B  C  D  E

43. __ __ __ __ __ __
   A  B  C  D  E  F

44. __ __ __ __ __
   A  B  C  D  E

45. __ __ __ __ __ __
   A  B  C  D  E  F

46. __ __ __ __ __
   A  B  C  D  E

47. __ __ __ __ __ __
   A  B  C  D  E  F

48. __
   __
   __
   __
   __

49. __
   __
   __
   __
   __
   __

50. __
   __
   __
   __

51. __
   __
   __
   __
   __

52. __
   __
   __
   __
   __
   __

53. __ __ __ percent

54. __ __ __ percent

55. __ __ __ percent

56. __ __ __ percent

57. __ __ __ __ __
   A  B  C  D  E

58. Please answer on
   back of answer
   sheet.

59. __ __
   A  B

60. __ __
   A  B

61. __ __ __
   A  B  C

62. __ __ __
   A  B  C

63. __ __
   A  B

64. __ __ __
   A  B  C

65. __ __ __
   A  B  C

66. __ __ __
   A  B  C

67. __ __ __ years

68. __ __ __ years

69. __ __
   A (Yes)  B (No)

70. Please answer
   back of answer
   sheet.

APPENDIX C

METHOD OF CONSTRUCTING INDEXES

In adding the results of different questions together in order to form
an index, we were concerned that one question not dominate an index, unless
that question was so important that it should be permitted to dominate other
questions in the index. For example, Questions 7 through 10 required
answers in percentages, from 0 to 100. Questions 1 and 2, on the other hand,
could be answered with alternatives A through E, with assigned scores of 1
through 5. If one wanted to compose an index containing Question 1 and
Question 7, one could not merely add the two questions together. Obviously,
answers in percentages would be higher numbers and the range in that question
would dominate any index composed by merely adding the two questions. If we
had decided in advance that Questions 1 and 7 should have the same weight in
the index, then we would look at the print-out of all answers for Question 7
(we never looked at cross-tabulations for groups) to determine the range of
answers. In this case, we found that answers ranged all the way from 0 to
100 percent. It was, therefore, feasible to reduce the range of the question
to 5 points by dividing the answers by 20. In the resulting transformation
of Question 7, the scores ranged from 0 to 5 (100 divided by 20). That range
was roughly equivalent to the range in Question 1.

An example of one question deserving a greater weight than another is
the weighting which we gave to Questions 3 and 4. Question 3 asks for the
number of insults. Question 4 asks for the number of threats or attempted

injuries. In advance, we decided that threats or attempts were three times more important than insults. These weights are subjective; however, in no case did we give any question more than three times the weight of any other question.

Sometimes, in order to make the range of a question roughly equal to the five points available in a multiple-choice question, we first reduced the possible score for extreme answers. For example, in Question 10, only 7 patrolmen thought that over 50 percent of the people in their precinct belonged to groups which support the police politically or as volunteers. Therefore, we imposed the constraint that the maximum score on this question would be 55.

Note that in the accompanying table each index begins with a constant. The purpose of the constant is to keep the index above zero. In general, our aim was to have the indexes approximate 100. No significance should be attached to the size of the number in an index. It is only possible to take significance from the differences among the scores on an index.

Note also that a shorthand has been used in the table for "values." The entries in the "value" column require some explanation. They represent, in an abbreviated form, specific steps that must be carried out. For instance, an entry of +1x indicates the following:

1.  Determine the score for the question.

2.  Carry out the indicated transformation (if any).

3.  Multiply the resulting number by 1(1x).

4.  Add (+) this number to the index.

Similarly, an entry of -3x indicates that the value for a question was transformed (if required), multiplied by 3, and then subtracted from the index.

TABLE C-1

| Index of Citizen Hostility | | |
|---|---|---|
| Source | Value | Transformations (if any) |
| Constant | +100 | |
| Question 3 | −x/6 | set all scores of 30 or more equal to 30. |
| Question 4 | −3x | set all scores of 5 or more equal to 5. |
| Question 8 | −x/5 | set all scores of 55 or more equal to 55. |
| Question 9 | −x/8 | set all scores of 50 or more equal to 50. |
| Question 19 | −3x | |
| Question 29 | −1x | |

| Index of Citizen Support | | |
|---|---|---|
| Constant | +100 | |
| Question 5 | +x/5 | set all scores of 25 or more to 25 and all scores of 1 or zero equal to zero |
| Question 6 | +x/4 | set all scores of 25 or more equal to 25 and all scores of 4 or less equal to 4. |
| Question 10 | +x/10 | set all scores of 50 or more equal to 50. |
| Question 17 | +2x | |
| Question 18 | +2x | |
| Question 31 | +1x | |

| Index of Distance of Average RMP Dispatch | | |
|---|---|---|
| Constant | +100 | |
| Question 37 | +1x | |
| Question 53 | −.4x | set all scores of 60 or more equal to 60. |
| Question 54 | −x/12 | |
| Question 55 | +x/16 | |
| Question 56 | +x/18 | |

TABLE C-1:  Continued

| Source | Value | Transformations (if any) |
|--------|-------|--------------------------|

### Index of Extrinsic (Pay, Schedule) Job Satisfaction

| Source | Value | Transformations (if any) |
|--------|-------|--------------------------|
| Constant | +105 | |
| Question 22 | -10x* | |
| Question 25 | -10x | |
| Question 26 | +20x | |

### Index of Citizen Willingness to Tempt Police With Favors

| Source | Value | Transformations (if any) |
|--------|-------|--------------------------|
| Constant | +107 | |
| Question 11 | -x/4 | set all scores of 60 or more equal to 60. |
| Question 12 | -3x | set all scores of 11 or more equal to 11. |

### Index of Perception of Change

| Source | Value | Transformations (if any) |
|--------|-------|--------------------------|
| Constant | +91 | |
| Question 10 | +1x | |
| Question 20 | +1x | |
| Question 21 | -1x | |
| Question 26 | +1x | |
| Question 34 | +1x | |

### Community-Crime-Control Attitude Index

| Source | Value | Transformations (if any) |
|--------|-------|--------------------------|
| Constant | +134 | |
| Question 47 | +3x | |
| Question 51 | +2x | count one each time item B, E, F, G, J, K, or T is listed. |
| Question 52 | -2x | count one each time item B, E, F. G. J, K, or T is listed. |
| Question 51 | -2x | count one each time item A, X, or Z is listed. |
| Question 52 | +2x | count one each time item A, X, or Z is listed. |
| Question 43 | -2x | |
| Question 46 | -2x | |
| Question 45 | -1x | |
| Question 44 | -1x | |
| Item 48A | +1x | count 1 if item is ranked first, 2 if item is ranked second, etc. |
| Item 50T | -1x | count 1 if item is ranked first, 2 if item is ranked second, etc. |
| Item 50Z | +1x | count 1 if item is ranked first, 2 if item is ranked second, etc. |

*This is the only index in which weights of ten and twenty were used.